WILLIAM IV, MRS. JORDAN,
AND THE FAMILY THEY MADE

Daniel A. Willis

Bygone Era Books

Copyright © 2011, Daniel A. Willis

Published by:
Bygone Era Books
7995 E. Eastman Ave. #B101
Denver, CO 80231

This book contains material protected under International and Federal Copyright Laws and Treaties. Any unauthorized reprint or use of this material is prohibited. No part of this book may be reproduced or transmitted in any form or by any means, electronic or mechanical, including photocopying, recording, or by any information storage and retrieval system without express written permission from the author.

ISBN: 978-1-941072-03-5

Printed in the United States of America

ALL RIGHTS RESERVED

TABLE OF CONTENTS

Preface	5
Chapter 1: King William IV	7
Chapter 2: Dorothy Bland, aka Mrs. Jordan	21
Chapter 3: The FitzClarences	31
Chapter 4: The Sidneys	49
Chapter 5: The Hays	61
Chapter 6: The Noels	77
Chapter 7: The Crichton-Stuarts	89
Chapter 8: The Duffs	97
Chapter 9: The Kennedy-Erskines	111
The Genealogy	117
Bibiography	189
Index	191

Preface

In recent decades, we have seen a great loosening of the restrictions against whom a member of the Royal Family may marry. All of the children of our current Queen have married, with permission, commoners, some more than once. This is a relatively recent change in attitude. It was only as recently as the children of the King George V, that marriage to a foreign Princess was not required for a son of the King.

Imagine for a moment if this more relaxed attitude had been in effect in 1790, and William, Duke of Clarence, third son of King George III, were allowed to marry the woman with whom he chose to live in domestic bliss. Had this happened, the lady we currently call Queen Elizabeth II, would be merely Mrs. Philip Mountbatten, and the Sovereign would be the relatively unknown man now known as Patrick Elborough.

But who is Patrick Elborough you may ask? He is the heir-general, albeit through an illegitimate line, of King William IV and his 20-year paramour, Dorothea Bland (aka Mrs. Jordan, the actress). But Mr. Elborough is only one of roughly 900 people who descend from this union of Prince and Actress. This book will seek to introduce the reader to the rest of them.

Other prominent figures who will appear in these pages include the current Prime Minister, David Cameron; television presenter, Adam Hart-Davis; his literarily well-known father, Sir Rupert; a recent Grand Master of the Sovereign Order of Malta as well as the current Grand Prior of England; race-car driver Johnny (7th Marquess of) Bute; and a flurry of statesman, nobles, and maybe even a royal or two.

Every effort has been made to verify every fact mentioned in this book. There will be, without a doubt, errors. They are the nature of the beast when covering large numbers of people and more than 200 years of a family. For these, please accept my apologies at this time.

Daniel Willis
Denver, Colorado
March, 2011

Chapter 1: King William IV

On August 21, 1765, the world was on the brink of great change. The Holy Roman Emperor, husband of the remarkable Empress Maria Theresa, had died a few days previously. Mozart was changing the way the world viewed music. And the British parliament was about to pass the Stamp Act on the American Colonies, which proved to be the catalyst for the movement that culminated in the War of American Independence.

It was into this world that Britain's Queen Charlotte, with little fanfare, was delivered of a third healthy son, to be named William Henry. By this point, George III already had his "heir and a spare" in his older boys, George (later King George IV) and Frederick (later Duke of York), so while a third son was no less welcome, he was also not nearly as prized as the elder two. In time, the King and Queen would become the parents of fifteen children, all but two of whom would survive to adulthood.

Prince William's early childhood was spent in almost constant companionship with his elder brothers at Kew House, some eleven miles up the Thames from Westminster. In 1772, the elder boys were given establishments of their own so William's education took place with his next younger brother, Edward (later Duke of Kent and father of Queen Victoria). Dr. Majendie, a Hugenot descendant from Exeter, had originally been given the job of governor for all of the young princes, but when they were separated, he remained with William and Edward. Majendie was assisted by General Bude, a Dutchman whose rank derived from military experience in the offices of high command rather than on the battlefield proper.

King George lived a rather austere life, especially when compared to the opulent courts of Versailles, Madrid, or Vienna. He expected the same frugality of his children. Meals were often simple but nourishing and outdoor exercise was plentiful. Discipline was the order of the day. The children were usually not permitted to sit in their parents' presence, and outfits were to be meticulously cared for, as was their own personal appearance. In a day when children of the upper crust were generally kept out of sight of their parents, King George and Queen Charlotte actually gave a lot of attention to their children, and seem to have genuinely enjoyed their company, at least while they were young.

As Prince William grew, a problem developed: what to do with him. The eldest son's path in life was destined from birth, the second son typically was given over to the military, but a surviving third son was something of an anomaly in the Royal Family. King George himself had two younger brothers, but was very disappointed in both and felt theirs were wasted lives. Now he was faced with finding things to occupy six sons as Edward was followed by Ernest, Augustus and Adolphus. William was his first foray into this uncharted water of healthy younger sons. As it had already been determined that Frederick would pursue a career in the Army, William was given over to the Navy. This turned out to be a splendid match as William's temperament was well suited for a life at sea.

Midshipman William Guelph, as he preferred to be called, took his name from the ancient House to which his family belonged before their acquisition of Brunswick, and later Hanover, centuries earlier. It was a rather amazing piece of history that allowed the Hanovers to arrive at the British Throne at all. During the reign of the Tudors in the 16th century, many a battle was fought over the question of religion. It was, of course, Henry VIII, who had established the Church of England, and his children who battled royally over whether it should be a Catholic Church or a Protestant one. The Anglican form of Protestantism won out in the end and was pretty firmly established by the time James II ascended the Throne in 1685. However, James was married to the very Catholic Maria of Modena, and his heirs were being brought up as Catholics.

The parliament of the day was determined the Realm would remain Protestant, and so invited the King's son-in-law, the Prince of Orange, to overthrow James in the name of his wife Mary, who was James' eldest daughter by his first, and more importantly, Protestant, wife, Anne Hyde. The Prince staged what is remembered to history as the Glorious Revolution of 1688, placing himself and his wife jointly on the Throne as King William III and Queen Mary II. It was during William's reign that parliament passed the Act of Settlement, which established that the Kingdom would be ruled by a non-Catholic Sovereign forevermore. Under the new law, the Crown passed from William (whose wife Mary had predeceased him) to Anne, Mary's younger sister. Upon Queen Anne's death in 1714, dozens of Catholics were passed over to find a religiously appropriate heir.

Ultimately the Crown went to the descendants of James I's youngest daughter, Queen Elizabeth of Bohemia, whose youngest surviving daughter, Sophia, was married to the Elector of Hanover. The Electress Sophia missed becoming Queen herself by dying a mere two weeks before Queen Anne. Therefore, it was Sophia's eldest son who ascended the British Throne, as King George I, and was the great-grandfather of George III.

By the time Prince William joined the Navy in 1779, a mere lad of not quite fourteen, the Hanovers had successfully ruled the Kingdom for 65 years and crushed the last dregs of support for the Catholic descendants of King James II (called Jacobites). The pressing military matter of the day was the War of American Independence, still being waged across the Atlantic. The Prince's first taste of Navy life was aboard the *HMS Prince George*, a 98-gun warship, which joined the battle in America.

Much of William's naval career was spent carrying out the more mundane day-to-day tasks necessary to maintaining a ship at sea. He took to these chores with delight and insisted on being treated as any other midshipman and not as a Prince. However, being the son of the King, this could be accomplished only to a degree. Being as young as he was, William continued to have a tutor, even on shipboard. He was accompanied at sea by Rev. Henry Majendie, the son of his childhood governor at Kew House.

Once arriving at America, William's ship was briefly docked at New York, then still in the hands of loyalists. There were reports that Gen. George Washington was plotting to kidnap the Prince, and offer to make him King of a newly independent country. Looking at the situation with the 20/20 vision that hindsight offers, it seems more likely this plan was suggested to Washington by some of his officers, but that it was rejected. Just as well, as it would have been out of character for William to even entertain such a conspiratorial notion.

After a year and a half of two-to-three month cruises, broken up by brief visits to Kew, Prince William found himself at Windsor in time for the Christmas holidays of 1780. It had been during his time at sea that one of the greatest trials that a man faces hit full force: puberty. Now being on land, and no doubt prompted by his womanizing elder brothers, William had the opportunity to discover the opposite sex. For the next several years, the Prince would fall in and out of love with women of varying degrees of propriety, but none of which came close to the standards to be an appropriate wife. Therefore, William lived two love lives, one of properly conducted courtly pursuit, without capture, of nice girls and another of downright debauchery, reserved for the prostitutes of various ports-of-call. It became all too apparent to the King that William was following in the steps of his elder brothers in his love of sex, so it was decided to keep William at sea as much as possible.

For all of this time at sea, and not having seen much action during the war with the United States, William was not advancing in rank very fast. The King, in his efforts to control the amount of time William was on land, purposely held him back. This finally came to a head in 1790, when William demanded, unsuccessfully, his own command and ultimately resigned from the Navy, ironically being promoted to Rear-Admiral upon his retirement.

Having been created the Duke of Clarence the year previously, William now began living a life of courts and balls, along with many other members of his family. This included incursions into Parliament, usually defending the payment of the Prince of Wales's ever increasing debts.

William's financial issues were never as severe as his eldest brother's, but he lived in debt much of his single life. He was a very generous man and insisted on his guests always being as comfortable as possible. This comfort usually came at a price higher than his stipend from Parliament allowed.

This fateful winter of 1789-90 was momentous for another reason. It was the season William met the celebrated actress, Mrs. Jordan, which was the stage name of Dorothea Bland. Within the year a full fledged affair had begun, and their first child, George, was born in 1794. Over the course of the next sixteen years, Dora, as she was known to her intimates, would produce another nine children for the Duke, who were all duly recognized and surnamed FitzClarence.

William very happily settled into a comfortable domestic life with Dora and the children. This unorthodox family, which included Dora's children from previous relationships, melded into a blissful tribe, centered at Bushy Park, on the grounds of Hampton Palace. Bushy Park would be William's residence for the next twenty years. The subsequent chapters of this book will be devoted to Dora, the FitzClarence clan, and their descendants.

William's post-Dora life had further adventures. A short time after the birth of their last child, William faced, in addition to his approaching 50th birthday, what we now would call a "mid-life crisis," complete with the wandering eye, and less resistance of the body to follow. There was also pressure from his family to find a royal wife. By this point, there was only one eligible British grandchild of King George III to succeed to the Throne: Princess Charlotte of Wales. The remainder of the grandchildren were either illegitimate or members of foreign royal houses. William and Dora had an amicable break-up. Legal papers were drawn up to ensure proper care of the children, and it was all finalized by early 1812. Dora only lived on until 1815, dying impoverished, mostly due to her own generosity, in the south of France.

In 1817, a tragedy occurred which caused all of the royal brothers to step up the pace towards the altar. Princess Charlotte of Wales, only child of the Prince Regent (after 1820, King George IV) died, along with her baby, in childbirth. This event placed William directly in the crosshairs to become King, as his second eldest brother, the Duke of York, was childless and married to a Duchess who had passed child-bearing age.

The quest for a Princess to wed was slow and tedious. William, now 52, and already with a family of ten illegitimate children, was not a prize catch for young Princesses who were still chaste and pure. Arrangements were finally made, with significant help from all of his family, for him to marry the 25-year-old Princess Adelaide of Saxe-Meiningen. And just for good measure, the 1818 wedding would be a double ceremony with his next younger brother, the Duke of Kent, who had picked as his bride the widowed Princess of Leiningen, born Princess Victoria of Saxe-Coburg. To round out the marriages of the sons of George III, the Duke of Cumberland married, in 1815, their first cousin, Duchess Frederica of Mecklenburg. The youngest surviving son, the Duke of Cambridge, married Princess Augusta of Hesse-Cassel only a few days before William's marriage. The next to youngest son, the Duke of Sussex, proved to be the marital black sheep of the family. He entered into two alliances which did not conform to the Royal Marriages Act, therefore being declared illegal. Both would-be brides were from the British nobility and were perfectly nice ladies, but King George (and later William himself) would not grant permission for a marriage to a non-royal.

The new Duchess of Cambridge was immediately accepting of the large brood of FitzClarences which now lived with their father, their mother already being dead. It is probably good that William had so many children on which Adelaide could lavish her love and care, since her own children both died as newborns. In later years, all of William's children would remark on the extraordinary efforts made by their step-mother to make them feel loved, and to be sure they were properly introduced into society. The Queen, as Adelaide became in 1837, also helped her step-children find and make appropriate matches.

Old George III finally died in 1820, having long since been locked up as a lunatic, followed by his eldest son and heir, George IV, only ten years later. By the time of George IV's death in 1830, the Duke of York was already dead, so the Throne fell to William. After 64 years of having his life controlled by his father and brother, William accepted the crown with maybe a tad more glee than was respectful of his dead brother. Nonetheless, the seven-year reign of William IV had begun.

King William IV had done so much living during his time as Prince, that his reign as King was somewhat anti-climatic, although there was one major piece of legislation passed due to the King's direct influence. The Reform Bill of 1832 addressed what had become inequities in the country's electoral system, a system that had been unchanged since Tudor days. But getting the Reform Bill passed was more of a challenge than anyone had anticipated. William was faced with several difficult choices regarding Parliament during this period which led him to dissolve it at one point for fresh elections, and at another point, to personally admonish the House of Lords on their failure to pass the Reform Bill. Other laws passed during his reign, though without his personal input, were the abolition of slavery in the Colonies, and greater restrictions on child labor.

The year 1834 brought another round of disagreement between King and Parliament, and eventually the King dissolved parliament, again triggering new elections which did not go as the King had hoped. Parliament sent their choice of Prime Minister to the King, but he refused Lord Melbourne a second stint, instead selecting a Tory, Sir Robert Peel. Peel's administration never had a chance, as Melbourne's party was in control of the House of Commons. Ultimately Melbourne was restored as Prime Minister and continued as such for the remainder of William's reign.

King William and Queen Adelaide spent much of their reign trying to develop a friendship with, and to mentor, his niece and heir, Princess Victoria of Kent. These efforts were thwarted by Victoria's mother, the Duchess of Kent. The Duchess, for her part, had always gone to great lengths to shield her daughter from her paternal uncles as she viewed them all as lecherous old men. Though this assessment may have been accurate, the result lead to young Victoria ascending a Throne she was not groomed for. Fortunately, her ministers were well prepared for this situation, and she did just fine, having a Great Age of history named for her.

William IV died of a heart-attack, without much fuss or muss, just as he would have wanted, on the 20th of June, 1837, ending the Hanoverian era that had lasted since 1714. He was buried in the Royal Crypt at Windsor Castle where much of his family rests. Queen Adelaide lived on until the end of 1849. She was always remembered for the kindness she showed others, particularly her numerous step-children, and ever-growing army of step-grandchildren. Queen Victoria was always very fond of this aunt and remembered her when naming her own first daughter, Victoria Adelaide Mary Louise (later the German Empress). Her subjects also remembered the Dowager Queen fondly and named Adelaide, Australia, that country's only large interior city, after her.

Chapter 2: Dorothy Bland, aka Mrs. Jordan

If William IV was born into the pampered world of royalty, the mother of his surviving children was reared in the exact opposite. Dorothea "Dora" Bland was born in 1761 to parents whose own marriage was "everything but legal." Her father, Francis Bland, had parents devoted to religious service and not willing to accept aspiring actress, Grace Phillips, into their family, so a marriage was never performed. Francis and Grace simply lived away from his family "as if married" for appearances sake.

Dora was the third child of the Bland household, having an elder brother, George, and sister, Hester. The total number of children born to Grace has not been accuturately recorded, but is believed to be in the ballpark of nine, the last of whom was born in early 1774. Most of this time was spent in Dublin, where Grace was able to find work acting on a more or less regular basis.

One of the great disadvantages of not having a marriage certificate is that one cannot legally force a spouse to remain with the family or remit compensation if he doesn't. Thus, in 1774 Francis Bland left his "wife" and children, married an heiress and began a new family with the legal wife. Francis Bland did little to support his first family after this point, so it made little difference that he only lived four more years.

It was about this time that Dora began her own remarkable odyssey on the stage. She started in Dublin, following her mother's path. Just to be working, she initially tried out for all sorts of productions, both tragedy and comedy, but early on showed a genuine talent for the comedic roles. She quickly found herself in lead roles and working in Dublin's better theatres.

In 1780, Dora had the misfortune to begin performing in a theatre owned by Richard Daly. A year or so later, during their second season, he seduced her. It is generally accepted that this seduction was anything but romantic, with accounts ranging from what today would be called sexual harassment to outright rape. Whatever the true circumstances were, Dora removed herself from Daly's presence as soon as she could manage it, but not before finding herself pregnant with his child. In due course, Dora's first child, Frances, known as Fanny, was born.

Dora was an especially affectionate mother, but once Fanny reached adulthood, their relationship was stormy on the best of days. It is easy to imagine Dora resenting a child who was begotten in such an odious manner, but her biographers have generally agreed she made every effort to not punish Fanny for the crimes of her father.

Dora's life after Richard Daly improved considerably. Moving back to England with her mother and siblings in tow, she found work in Yorkshire with a chain of theatres owned by Tate Wilkinson. It was he who named her "Mrs. Jordan." The name was a biblical reference, just as she had crossed the water from Ireland to be free of Daly, it was as if she had crossed the River Jordan into a Promised Land. It was by this pseudonym that she would be known the rest of her life.

As her reputation as a great actress continued to blossom, she made, in 1785, the inevitable migration to London's Drury Lane, then the center of the theatrical world. It was here that she met and fell in love with Richard Ford a year later. The next three years were to bring relative personal happiness, a successful and profitable professional life, and three more children: Dorothea "Dodee" in 1787, a baby boy who sadly only lived a few hours in 1788, and Lucy in 1789. However, 1789 also saw the beginning of a lot of change for Mrs. Jordan.

In July of that year, Dora's devoted mother, Grace, passed away, leaving several of Dora's siblings in her care in addition to the three children of her own to raise. She had tried for three long years to nail Richard down on the prospect of marriage but he always managed to escape the noose. And this was the year that she caught the eye of a royal admirer: Prince William, the Duke of Clarence.

The Duke soon began efforts to woo Dora, but kept a respectable distance in public, as she was generally thought of as married to Richard Ford. In the meanwhile, Dora stepped up her efforts to get the ever-elusive legal marriage from Richard. He continued to hesitate and finally Dora delivered an ultimatum in early 1791: the Duke wanted her and would have her if Ford wouldn't marry her. Ford let her go.

From the get go, there was an understanding that William would never be able to marry Dora. He could and would be devoted and faithful to her, but the Royal Marriages Act made a marriage out of the question. Dora seems to have been very accepting of these conditions and soon moved in with the Duke. Prior to this arrangement, Dora had purchased a home in the Petersham district of London called Somerset House. It was here that the first two of her ten children with William would be born. The remainder were all born at Bushy House.

Bushy House was a royal residence that was provided for William in his titular role as Park Warden for Bushy Park, which is near Hampton Court. It was somewhat run down as it had been uninhabited for several years, but William and Dora set about putting it to rights and even adding a bit to the original buildings. Here, Dora again found herself in an "all but legal" marital relationship, now with the Duke.

Finances were always a major issue in Dora's life, as well as William's. When they got together, William was horribly in debt. This was mostly due to being a Prince. He was expected to entertain and live in a certain manner, one that was well outside the annual allowance Parliament was willing to provide. He often turned to his father for debt-relief, with mixed results. Dora, for her part, had been the primary money maker for much of her family, which included three children and three unwed sisters when she took up with the Duke. She also had cared for her mother until the latter's death. Yet she demonstrated a good head for money and actually helped her royal lover get his own debt under control.

The Clarence household was generally buoyed by Dora's continuing income as an actress. She continued to work through nearly the entirety of her relationship with William. If the Duke was not happy with this arrangement, he did not fuss about it. He was no doubt all too happy to have the income. As the family grew, this became even more important.

The Duke of Clarence and Mrs. Jordan would go on to have ten children together between 1794 and 1807, all surnamed FitzClarence. As the family continued to grow, and domestic bliss reigned supreme at Bushy House, even the most ardent opponents to this unorthodox royal arrangement were quelled. Dora began finding herself welcome in the highest social circles and often accompanied her lover to major social events. Even old King George III and Queen Charlotte came to appreciate the calming influence Dora had on their sometimes wayward son. They accepted these illegitimate grandchildren in their own way in private, but maintained a public distance in Court life.

Dora Jordan was well known to all as a devoted and loving mother. Nearly every farthing she earned went to their care, ultimately to her ruin. Between her and their royal father, the FitzClarence children received top-notch educations and, when their age dictated, were introduced into the best social circles. Some followed the Hanoverian tradition of being quarrelsome with their parents, but never to the point of a complete rupture within the family.

Eventually, Dora's remaining sisters married and went off to live their own lives. Her brother George remained an active part of her life. Of her children born prior to meeting the Duke, Fanny Daly married Thomas Alsop, a general waste of the flesh and blood it took to make him; Dodee Ford married Fred Marsh, the conniving illegitimate son of Lord Henry FitzGerald, himself a son of the Duke of Leinster; and Lucy Ford married a Colonel Hawker, moving with him to his various posts throughout the Empire.

By 1811, four years after their final child was born, Prince William had become restless in this not-quite-legal domestic situation. It was increasingly apparent that there might be a real chance for him to ascend the Throne, despite being the third son. His elder brothers were in their fifties and not likely to father any more children with their wives, and only one child survived: Princess Charlotte, daughter of the eldest brother, George (later King George IV). Furthermore, pressure from his family to marry a foreign Princess and make more heirs was mounting. Finally he decided to split with Dora.

In December 1811, a formal arrangement of separation was drawn up, with an allowance going to Dora for herself and each of her younger children until they reached age 13, at which point they would go to live with William. One provision that seemed out of character for the Duke, and was likely insisted upon by the Regent's advisors, required Dora to forfeit her allowance if she returned to the stage as a working actress. She had by this time been in a state of semi-retirement.

Dora left Bushy House in February 1812, having bought herself a house in Cadogan Place. Within the year, she found herself financially required to return to the stage giving up her allowance from William. She continued working until 1814, when she left the stage, never to return. Her last performance turned into an impromptu retirement party with the theatre packed to the rafters with well-wishers and not a dry eye in the house.

Unfortunately, even with her income from the stage, she could not keep up with her debts, many of which were created by her generosity to her children. Even though the older children were now married and theoretically on their own, she found she was usually still the one keeping them out of the poor house.

In 1815, she discovered her ne'er-do-well son-in-law, Fred Marsh had been spending her money and raising debt in her name. She soon found herself hounded by debt collectors for amounts she had no hope of paying off. She retained legal counsel to help with the debt situation and was advised to move to the Continent so the debt collectors could not reach her, and to allow her lawyers some time to gather proof that Fred had fraudulently been raising her debt.

She moved to Boulogne, France, her house and belongings having now been seized and auctioned off at well below their value. Little is recorded of her last months in France. She wrote to her children regularly, but the letters have not survived. Her health apparently deteriorated rapidly, and Dora Bland, known to the world as Mrs. Jordan, died in a very cheap rental on July 5th, 1816, aged 55, completely destitute and alone. What little she had left was sold off and her debts were paid at the rate of five shillings to the pound.

Her grave in St. Cloud went unmarked until her children found out and erected a simple tombstone for her. She is buried in a corner of a small churchyard, nearly as lonely as she died. There is irony worthy of Shakespeare in that the greatest comedic actress of her day ended life in such tragic circumstances.

Chapter 3: The FitzClarences

In the thirteen year interval between 1794 and 1807, Mrs. Jordan bore 10 healthy children to the Duke of Clarence. All of these children would grow to adulthood. It was tradition in the day for illegitimate children to take as a surname Fitz plus their father's name. So a child of Gerald would be named FitzGerald. The children of William and Dora though were named FitzClarence in reference to their father's title rather than his name.

The children were generally raised at Bushy Park, near Hampton Court. This more rural setting provided not only a physically healthy environment to grow in, but also afforded a certain amount of privacy for a family that was not quite proper. The press had been particularly cruel in their depictions of William and Dora's arrangement in the beginning. Once it became apparent that this was going to be a lasting relationship, they quieted down a bit.

The first born child was named George, after the Prince of Wales, to whom William was always devoted. William had been somewhat on the outs with his parents for quite some time at this point, so perhaps this was his way of sticking his tongue out at them. George and his next younger brother, Henry, were the only children of William and Dora not to be born at Bushy Park. They were both born at Dora's home in Petersham.

George was educated at Harrow, as were all of his brothers, and was an average student. He would later show interest in Asian military history, travelling extensively throughout the Far East as a young man. He collected and amassed a large catalogue of information from libraries all over the European and Asian continents whichhe published, 1817, as *A History of the Art of War among Eastern Nations* to very favorable reviews from the halls of academia. He followed this up by publishing a book about his travels, *Journal of a Route Across India*, a year later.

With an income from his books, he was able to start a family and did so by marrying Mary Wyndham, an illegitimate daughter of the 3rd Earl of Egremont. One would think George and Mary would have been well suited to each other as they both came from non-traditional families and understood the various societal inconveniences that situation handed them. The marriage produced seven children, although one lived only a month. However happy the marriage started, it did not continue that way, George often finding other sleeping accommodations.

Like so many men in the Hanover family, George felt it was his duty, as eldest son, to be the most quarrelsome with his father. Early on, these quarrels were often over money. Both William and Dora provided their children an adequate upbringing. It was not as opulent as William himself had experienced, but it was not exactly frugal either. When William and Dora separated in 1811, George embarked on a resentment of his father that was never alleviated.

However, this did not stop William, who was now King, from using his newfound royal powers in 1830 to do all he could to help his firstborn[1]. He gave him some royal

---

[1] William reportedly had fathered one other son prior to his relationship with Dora, by an unknown lady. This child supposedly

functions to carry out and, three months prior to his coronation, created George the 1st Earl of Munster, a secondary title that William himself had carried prior to his ascension. Even this led to a bitter row between father and son as George, being the King's eldest son, believed he should have a role in the coronation ceremony. Decorum of the day, as well as the Archbishop of Canterbury who oversaw the ceremony, simply would not permit it.

In an effort to appease his son, William made him a member of the Privy Council. This was not for George, who found himself estranged from Court for much of his father's reign. Queen Victoria, always rather fond of the FitzClarence clan, made him her aide-de-camp until 1841 when he seems to have again fallen out of favor. His bitter resentment of his life in general, his unhappy marriage, and his bleak financial situation finally got the better of him on 20 March 1842 when he shot himself, using a pistol presented to him by his uncle and namesake, King George IV, when the latter was Prince of Wales. George's estranged wife followed him to the grave

---

He was also named William, however evidence of his existence is fleeting. According to Tomalin, this child died in the Navy at sea in late 1806 or early 1807.

that December. They were survived by their six remaining children, two girls and four boys, ranging in age from 6 to 22.

The eldest child, a daughter named Adelaide in honor of William's Queen, lived a quiet life away from Court and never married. She died at the age of 63. Her only surviving sister, Augusta, fell in love with a handsome Swedish diplomat, Baron Bonde, while studying in Paris. She eloped to Sweden where they lived at the Bonde estate in Grimmersta. Sadly Augusta's happiness was short lived. She died in 1846, less than a week after delivering a healthy daughter named in her memory.

The younger Baroness Augusta Bonde grew up in Grimmersta with her father, who remarried to Helena Robinson, another English girl, perhaps to replace the mother little Augusta had lost. Augusta made a brilliant matrimonial coup by marrying Gustave Fouché, the heir of the Duke of Otrante, Sweden's wealthiest noble at the time. But, like her mother, Augusta's married life was cut short by her death in 1872. Also like her mother, she left a young daughter, this one named Augustine, later Mrs. Frederik Peyron. The Peyron descendants immigrated to the United States in the middle of the 20th century and are now settled there in New England.

The eldest son of the Earl of Munster was named William in 1824, despite his father's ongoing disagreements with the child's namesake and grandfather. William succeeded his father as Earl in 1842. Having also been educated at Harrow, William sought a military career, serving in the Life Guards until he retired as a Captain upon his succession to the peerage. In 1855, he married his first cousin, Wilhelmina Kennedy-Erskine, daughter of his father's sister, Augusta. They also had a large family of seven boys and two girls.

The first two sons of the 2nd Earl both died young, as did the fourth son, leaving the third son, Geoffrey to inherit the title. Like his father, he was also a career military man, serving in the 1879–80 Afghan War, and the Boer War a year afterwards. He later fought in the South African War of 1899-1902, where he earned the Distinguished Service Order (DSO). Having survived many military campaigns, he was killed in a mining accident, unmarried, while still in South Africa in 1902.

The fifth son, Aubrey, also a bachelor, succeeded Geoffrey as the 4th Earl. He carried the title with little distinction and, having remained unmarried, passed it on, upon his death in 1928, to the son of his youngest brother,

Harold. Being sixth and seventh sons, there was no reason to believe either William or Harold FitzClarence would ever inherit the title. But, had William not succumbed to "jungle fever" in Africa in 1899, he would have done just that. Although he did marry, William produced only daughters, so the titles were not able to go to his descendants.

William FitzClarence's elder daughter, Dorothy, named in honor of her famous ancestress, married Cadogan Elborough, in 1909, and had five children over the next eleven years. Today, the Elboroughs are quite numerous, living in pockets around England. One of the younger generation has immigrated to Hawaii, where he is now building his own family. This family is headed up by Patrick, born in 1937. He caught the attention of the media in 1981, when an industrious reporter figured out he would be the King had William IV and Mrs. Jordan married.

William FitzClarence's younger daughter, Wilhelmina, married in 1918 to Cecil Maunsell, a Justice of the Peace and Lord of Rothwell Manor in Kettering, Northamptonshire. Their only child was Cecilia, first wife of George Kennard, who would later become the last Baronet of that name. George married another royal descendant as his fourth wife, Georgina Werhner, a granddaughter of Grand Duke Michael of Russia. George and Cecilia's daughter, Zandra, now approaching 70, has been married since 1962 to John Powell and is a noted artist living near Kettering. She has two grown children and three school-aged grandchildren.

The 2nd Earl's seventh son, Harold, followed the "family business" by joining the military, ultimately achieving the rank of Major. He married Frances Keppel, a scion of the Earl of Albemarle's family, in 1902. They had two children: Joan and Geoffrey. Lady Joan, having been raised to the rank of an Earl's daughter in 1928, married Oliver Birkbeck, of an old landed family from Norfolk. In her widowhood, Joan remarried to Henry Cator, a man 18 years her junior.

Lady Joan's younger brother, Geoffrey, succeeded his uncle as Earl in 1928. Geoffrey Munster, as he was commonly called, followed a career in politics. After taking a seat in the conservative benches in the House of Lords, he was appointed a Lord-in-Waiting, as well as the government whip in the Lords, during the Macdonald, Baldwin and Chamberlin governments. When World War II broke out, he moved to the State Department, where he started as Paymaster General but soon moved up to Undersecretary of State for War. After the war, he continued to hold several high-ranking positions within government, mostly dealing with the Colonies. He ultimately died in 1975, leaving a widow, the former Hilary Wilson, but - like many of his predecessors, - no children. His title would go to a second cousin.

The two daughters of the 2nd Earl of Munster, Ladies Lillian and Dorothea, each married in the 1890s and each had two children. Lillian married William Boyd and Dorothea married Chandos Lee-Warner. But these two lines quickly became extinct, as none of their children had any children of their own. Lillian's daughter, Phyllis, was the only one of them to marry. Her husband was a French nobleman, Vicomte Henri de Janzé, brother of the Comte de Janzé. The Comte figures into the tail of another William IV descendant, as he was the ex-husband of a mistress of the 22nd Earl of Erroll.

The second son of the 1st Earl, the Hon. Frederick FitzClarence, was born in 1826 and, after marrying his first cousin, the Hon. Adelaide Sidney, added Hunloke to his surname. The Sidney family had become the heirs of the Hunloke family, which was now extinct in the male line. However, Fredrick and Adelaide had no children to whom to pass this name. It would devolve to a nephew of Adelaide's,

Sir Philip Hunloke. Between Frederick and his next younger brother, George, was a baby girl who survived only a few days.

While many of the FitzClarences pursued Army careers, George joined the Royal Navy and was raised to the rank of Captain. He married Lady Maria Scott, daughter of the 3rd Earl of Clonmell, and heiress of the estate, "Bishopscourt," in co. Kildare. The four sons of George and Maria, - Charles, Edward, William, and Lionel, - all joined the army, the elder two eventually being killed in action. The two daughters lived in relative obscurity, the younger, Mary, being the only one to marry. She and her husband, Frederick Wing, had only one child, Gertrude, who died an elderly, but unmarried, lady in 1983.

The eldest son, Charles, became the war hero of the family. Serving in Africa with a few different regiments late in the 19th century, he was decorated with the Victoria Cross for his bravery at Mafeking. Ultimately he was killed in action during World War I, in Ypres, France. His brother, Edward, was killed fighting with the Egyptian army in what is now the Sudan, while the youngest son, Lionel, died in the early days of World War II in the Crimea.

Only Charles and Lionel left descendants, the former's becoming the last Earls of Munster and the latter's being an only daughter, Mary, who lived a quiet life in Sussex with her Polish husband, Adam Gluskiewicz. Their only child, Anna, now a "lady of a certain age," has never married.

Charles' eldest son, Edward, eventually inherited the Earldom of Munster from his second cousin, Geoffrey, when he was already a 75-year-old man, but carried the title for eight years until his death in 1983. During his years as plain Mr. FitzClarence, he served in the Army during World War II in Egypt, mostly in a staff position, and married twice. His first marriage, to Monica Grayson, the daughter of a Baronet, played out in the years between the wars and produced his only children. A second marriage, to Vivian Scholfield, turned out to be much longer, lasting until his death.

The son of the 6th Earl was Anthony, 7th and last Earl of Munster. By the time of his death in 2000, all other branches of the FitzClarence family had become extinct in the male line. After being educated at St. Edward's School in Oxford, and in Switzerland, Tony FitzClarence joined the Royal Navy, at age 16 in 1942, and served until 1947, being wounded in action along the way.

Being from a junior line of the family in his early adulthood, Tony had no real hereditary income of his own. After training at the Central School of Crafts and Arts in London, he began a career as a graphic designer, working for the Daily Mirror and then the Sun, finally working his way into being a sustainable freelancer. Later in life he developed an expertise in stained glass. After becoming Lord FitzClarence and heir to the Earldom, he took first a staff position at the Burrell Collection in Glasgow, and later with Chapel Studio.

His marital career was as varied as his professional one, having had four wives: Diane Delvigne, Pamela Hyde, Alexa Maxwell, and Halina Winska. The first and last wives survive today, as well as his four daughters, two from each of his first two wives. The last Countess of Munster also has a daughter from a previous relationship, who assumed the FitzClarence name.

Tony's eldest daughter, Lady Tara, is married to Ross Heffler and has two college-aged children. The second daughter, Lady Finola, divorced her husband of 25 years, Jonathan Poynton, in 2007. The couple had two children of their own, who are also in their twenties. The third daughter, born with the name Oonaugh, was born two years prior to the marriage of her parents and was shortly thereafter adopted by John Lawrence Mills. Now known as Charlotte Lawrence Mills, she is married to Raymond Burt and has three children. The youngest daughter, Lady Georgina, married briefly to Paul Phillips before remarrying to John Adam and having one son by the latter.

Tony's only sibling was his sister, Lady Mary-Jill, who died rather young at age 42, but not before she married twice. Perhaps it was a blessing she had no children to leave motherless.

Like his son, the 6th Earl also only had one sibling, a younger sister named Joan. Unlike her niece, though, Joan has descendants. She had married, in 1933, to Francis Barchard, who was later killed in World War II, leaving Joan with two young daughters, Jane and Elizabeth. Both have married and have had only daughters themselves. Now there are grandchildren ranging in age from teens on down.

Edward, the youngest son of the 1st Earl, like so many of his relatives, began a military career. However, his career and his life were cut tragically short as he was killed in action in the Crimean War in 1855, only two weeks after his eighteenth birthday.

The eldest daughter of Mrs. Jordan and the Duke of Clarence was Sophia, the apple of her father's eye nearly from birth. Her life and descendants will be discussed in the next chapter.

For all of the disagreement that Prince William had with his eldest son, he was a doting father to his second, named Henry Edward. Of all of their children, young Henry seems to have had the hardest time coping with the separation of his parents. It appears to be what motivated him to sign on to a campaign going to India. It was here that he learned of his mother's death in 1815, and also here that he met with a fatal illness himself two years later. Young Henry FitzClarence died without having been married, one of three of the FitzClarence children of King William IV not to produce additional descendants.

Lady Mary FitzClarence, the second daughter of the Duke of Clarence and Mrs. Jordan, was another of these three siblings. She married in 1824 to another notable bastard, Charles Richard Fox. Fox was the illegitimate son of the 3rd Baron Holland and his mistress, Lady Webster, whom he would later marry. Young Fox made his way through the ranks of the army, eventually becoming a general. After his military career, he entered politics, being a Whig MP for various constituencies in the 1830s and 40s. He was also a renowned collector of ancient Greek coins. After his death, his collection was sold to the royal museum in Berlin.

William and Dora's third son, Frederick, made the military his life's work. Most notably, he was the military governor of Portsmouth in the mid-19th century. He was a well respected administrator, with several plaques and monuments devoted to his memory. He married Augusta Boyle, a daughter of the 4th Earl of Glasgow, and by her had two daughters, one who died in infancy and another, who lived to adulthood, but did not marry.

The third daughter of William and Dora, Elizabeth, was to be the most prolific in terms of descendants. No fewer than four subsequent chapters will be devoted to the descendants of Lady Elizabeth FitzClarence and her husband, the 18th Earl of Erroll.

A hereditary insanity ran through several of the Hanoverian men. It has been most famously documented in King George III. However, the behavior of Lord Adolphus FitzClarence, William and Dora's fourth son, left little doubt he was of the same gene pool as "Mad King George." Lolly, as he was called by his mother, carried out a very respectable, even notable, naval career. But, the older he got, the more peculiar he became, often to the entertainment of his numerous nieces and nephews. His odder behavior was never a threat, and was generally tolerated by his family as all in good fun. Lolly FitzClarence never married, so if there was a hereditary taint, at least he didn't pass it along.

The next FitzClarence child, Augusta, was the progenitress of the Kennedy-Erskine line of descendants, more of whom we will meet in the last chapter.

The youngest son, Augustus, turned his energies toward the church. He ultimately became the Vicar of Mapledurham in Oxfordshire. He married Sarah Gordon, a granddaughter of the 9th Marquess of Huntly. They had six children, of whom, only Dorothea and Henry married.

Dorothea FitzClarence married Thomas Goff in 1863. Their only surviving descendants are through their granddaughter, also named Dorothea, who married Harold Swann. The Swann family is now also gone, as their only grandchildren were all daughters and have now married into other families. Henry FitzClarence's family has not proven as resilient. His son, Augustus, was killed in World War I, leaving no children. Henry's daughter, Cynthia, had two daughters of her own, by husband Roland Orred, but they too died childless.

For a family that started with ten children two hundred years ago, the FitzClarence name is all but gone at this point, being held only by the daughters of the last couple of Earls. However, many descendants in the female line remain. We will be exploring those lines in the next several chapters.

Chapter 4: The Sidneys

Having such a large number of children who were not royal, William and Dora gave the British nobility a rare opportunity to marry children of a King. Royal princes and princesses were generally expected to marry foreign royalty in the early 19th century as the noble classes of the home land were not considered good enough. However, since Mrs. Jordan's children were not royal in name, they were eligible, and very desirable, as spouses for British peers. And, not since the reign of Charles II, had a king provided such a bounty of children for them to choose from. In order to equate their rank to the nobles they hoped to marry, upon his ascension to the Throne, William elevated them all to the rank of a Marquess's child, save the eldest son who was given his own peerage title as the Earl of Munster.

William and Dora's eldest daughter, Sophia, was the apple of her father's eye. While he loved all his children, she presented the first opportunity for William to have a "daddy's little girl." This may have contributed to his allowance for her to marry for love to the heir of a mere Baronet, albeit a wealthy one, Philip Sidney.

Baronets can be best described as hereditary knighthoods. Their numbers are not considered peers, they do not sit in the House of Lords, and they are styled the same as a knight: Sir before their given name. However Baronets are not knights in the sense of belonging to any order of chivalry and rank in precedence above such knights except those of the Orders of the Garter and the Thistle.

So it was into this "neither Lord nor Knight" realm that Lady Sophia FitzClarence married in 1825. Philip's father, Sir John, had inherited the historic Penhurst Place, a 14th century manor house in Kent from his maternal ancestors, the Earls of Leicester. Penhurst has remained the seat of the Sidney family ever since. Now open to the public, some of its visage has been made famous by being used as a set for movies such as *The Princess Bride* and *The Other Boleyn*

Girl and is presently being used to represent Camelot in the BBC (SyFy Channel in the US) series *Merlin*.

After ten years of marriage, William, now King, saw fit to raise his son-in-law to the Peerage as Baron de L'Isle and Dudley. While there is little doubt this was done as a service to his daughter, publicly it was a reward for Sir Philip's service to the people as an MP from Eye followed by service to the Crown as the King's Equerry. After the creation he was also appointed a Lord of the Bedchamber, a particularly high post within the King's household.

The choice of titles was an acknowledgement of Sir Philip's ancestry. His ancestors, the Earls of Leicester, also held the title Viscount de L'Isle, and were themselves descended from Mary Dudley, sister of Elizabeth I's great love, Robert Dudley.

Within a year of her marriage, Sophia found herself giving birth to her first child, a daughter named Adelaide in honor of her step-mother, the future Queen Adelaide. The following decade would bring three more children: only son, Philip, in 1828; and daughters Ernestine and namesake Sophia in 1834 and 1837, respectively.

Like her husband, Sophia was appointed to a royal household position, Housekeeper of Kensington Palace. This does not mean she was cleaning the woodwork or polishing the silver. Housekeeper in this context refers to the person who manages the household staff and essentially keeps the palace running. In this position, Sophia was also able to keep her father apprised of the goings on there, as it was the home of William's heir, Princess Victoria of Kent. Young Victoria was generally kept away from her Hanoverian uncles by her widowed mother, deeming them all as unsavory influences. So, having a much loved and trusted daughter in the house was probably William's best source of information about his niece's upbringing.

Baroness de L'Isle died rather suddenly at the young age of 40 at Kensington Palace in April 1837. The loss of his favorite daughter likely prevented the King from rallying from his final heart attack. He followed her to the grave only two months later. Philip, her widowed husband, would live on to 1851, dying at Penhurst.

Philip Jr. led a reasonably quite life. Prior to succeeding his father, he was an officer in the Royal House Guards. When he became the 2nd Baron de L'Isle and Dudley in 1851, he took his seat in the conservative benches of the House of Lords. He married twice. His first wife, Mary Foulis, was the heiress of Ingleby Manor in Yorkshire. She was also the mother of all five of Philip's children before her sudden death in 1891. Two years, later he married Frances Ramsay, only to make her a widow five years after that.

Of Philip Jr.'s four sons, three would become Baron de L'Isle in their own turn. The only daughter, Mary, died unmarried at age 42, in 1903. She lived only seven years after the death of her unmarried brother, Henry.

The 3rd Baron, another Philip, did marry, to Elizabeth Vereker, daughter of the Viscount Gort, but they remained childless during their 20 years of marriage. This Philip was succeeded by his next younger brother Algernon who, remaining a bachelor, was succeeded in turn by the youngest brother, William, although the latter was only Baron for two months before his own death in June 1945.

When William Sidney, 5th Baron de L'Isle and Dudley died, he left two children by his wife, the former Winifred Yorke Bevan. These children were, by 1945, both married and had families of their own, but it was only that spring that an heir to the title was born.

William's daughter, Mary, who had married Walter Garnett in 1939, died prematurely a few days after her 53rd birthday, leaving a teenaged son.

Mary's brother, also named William, succeeded his father, in 1945, as the 6th Baron. By this time, he had already served with distinction in World War II, being wounded while fighting in France and Italy, earning him the Victoria Cross, Britain's highest military honor, for "showing valor in the face of the enemy." In later years when recounting his war record, if asked where he was shot, he would reply "in Italy" to avoid the embarrassment of talking about being shot in the buttocks.

After returning from the war, William quickly entered politics, being elected in 1944 to serve Chelsea in Parliament. The term only lasted a few months, as he succeeded to the Barony the following June. Steering his public service to a more diplomatic heading, the new Baron was appointed by Winston Churchill, to Secretary of State for Air, a position that oversaw the Royal Air Force before its incorporation into the Ministry of Defense. His efforts as veteran and Secretary were rewarded with an elevation in title to Viscount de L'Isle in 1956.

During his days in Churchill's cabinet he made a trip to Australia to research weapons production there and met often with that country's Prime Minister, Robert Menzies. When the position of Governor-General came open in 1961,

William was appointed to it, serving until retiring from public life in 1965.

On the home front, William had married, in 1940, the grand-niece of his Uncle Philip's wife, Jacqueline Vereker. They have five children, the middle one being his only son and heir, Philip, now the 2nd Viscount de L'Isle. The four daughters have, so far, racked up nine marriages among them, and mostly live in the London or Kent areas with their ever-growing numbers of grandchildren.

The current Viscount followed a military career until taking early retirement in 1979. Having succeeded his father in 1991, he was also appointed Vice-Lieutenant of Kent in 2002 and has since focused on the promotion of commerce for his ancestral home. He and his father were largely lauded for refurbishing Penhurst Place and its splendid gardens, now both open for the public to enjoy.

Viscount de L'Isle has been married since 1980 to the former Isobel Compton. The couple has two children named after their forebears, Sophia and Philip, and who are entering an age when it will soon be their turn to marry and continue the family lines.

Of the daughters of Lady Sophia FitzClarence and the 1st Baron de L'Isle, only Ernestine had children. However, the eldest daughter, Adelaide received an inheritance to pass on to them. Adelaide was determined to be the heiress to the last Hunloke Baronet who died in 1856. This inheritance included the 12th century manor house, Wingerworth, in Derbyshire. Adelaide and her husband, and cousin, Frederick FitzClarence, made Wingerworth their home until Frederick's death in 1878. Adelaide then moved back to London, putting the house up for rent.

Meanwhile, Adelaide's sister Ernestine had married Philip Perceval and began a family. Twins, Philip and Kathleen, were born in 1868 and wer followed by a sistes and a brother, of which, only the twins lived past the age of twenty. Kathleen died, unmarried, in 1931.

Philip Perceval thus became the heir to his childless aunt, Adelaide FitzClarence-Hunloke, who, with her husband, added the Hunloke name after their inheritance of that family's estate. As heir, Philip would change his name to Hunloke in 1904 upon Adelaide's death. In 1918, Philip returned to Wingerworth, but quickly found the expense of running such an estate to be beyond his means. He placed the manor up for sale, but without any takers, the house was eventually demolished in 1923.

Philip Perceval, as he was still named then, grew up at Villa Rothesay in London, near the water. He developed a love of sailing boats early on, starting a successful career in competitive sailing through the 1890s and on. In 1908, now named Hunloke, he represented Great Britain at the Olympic Games, bringing home a bronze medal in yachting. In 1914, he was appointed to royal service as a Groom-in-Waiting to King George V, moving on to becoming His Majesty's Sailing Master in 1920. Even in later life, he remained close to the sea, being a Commodore of the Royal Yacht Squadron from 1941 until his death in 1947.

Philip married, in 1892, to Silvia Heseltine, but his true wife remained the sea. In his authorized biography, which also doubled as a history of yachting, author Douglas Dixon did not even see fit to mention that Philip had a wife or children. But he did, - three children , in fact, - two daughters and a son to carry on the Hunloke name.

The elder daughter, Joan Hunloke, married the fabulously wealthy Philip Fleming of the Fleming banking family. He was also a cousin of Ian Fleming, creator of the famed spy, James Bond, as well as the beloved children's story, *Chitty Chitty Bang Bang*. Although the family has sold its share in the banking firm, they remain one of Britain's wealthiest families.

In recent years, the family has been in the news for another reason. Joan and Philip's grandson, Rory, entered into a high-profile society marriage with Denmark's Baroness Caroline Iuel-Brockdorff, herself a successful model. After seven years and two children, the couple began divorce proceedings. The protracted financial negotiations caused the divorce to drag on for quite some time, ultimately costing Rory Fleming a reported £400,000,000. For her part, Caroline has moved on to soccer star Niklas Bendtner, with whom she had a child at the end of 2010.

The Hunloke name was carried on by Philip and Silvia's son, Henry, and, after his death in 1978, his sons Timothy and Nicholas, the younger of whom is married with children and grandchildren. The Hunlokes have continued to marry well through the 20th century and to a smattering of British nobles. Henry's first wife, and mother of his sons, was Lady Anne Cavendish, daughter of the 9th Duke of Devonshire. Their only daughter, Philippa, married the 3rd Viscount Astor.

Nicholas, the current head of the family, is married to Lady Katherine Montagu, daughter of the 10th Earl of Sandwich, and their elder daughter, Henrietta, is married to a grandson of the 6th Marquess of Bath. Not bad for the descendants of a Drury Lane actress who started off on the wrong side of the blanket.

Chapter 5: The Hays

Lady Elizabeth FitzClarence, 3rd daughter of King William, is probably the only daughter to have been generally thought ill of. In 1824, and only at the age of 23, she was summed up by one her of contemporaries as "a domestic, lazy, fat, woman."[2] That was a pretty harsh appraisal of a daughter of the heir-presumptive to the Throne and wife of one of Scotland's premiere Peers.

In 1820, Elizabeth had married William Hay, the 18th Earl of Erroll. The Hay family is ancient enough to have their beginnings told in myth. The story goes that they descended from a farm worker who sent his sons to block the way of a retreating 11th century Scottish army forcing them to

---

[2] Gibbs, Vicary. *The Complete Peerage*. vol. VI, p.102

return to battle with the invading Danes ultimately winning the day. It is an interesting story, but more likely a later invention. There were, however, several true stories of the family's brave and gallant service to the Kings of Scotland in the 14th and 15th centuries. The Earls of Hay also serve as the hereditary High Constables of Scotland, a position which places them second only to the Royal Family in Scottish precedence.

By the time we get to the early 19th century, the Earls of Erroll of settled into just another noble Scots family of no particular distinction. They made their seat at Slains Castle near Cruden Bay in Aberdeenshire. Built in 1597 by the 9th Earl, the building was in bad need of repair by the 1830's and William made a complete overhaul. The Castle remained with the Hays until 1916, by which time financial misfortune forced them to sell the castle. The buyers also had to abandon the property and removed the roof to avoid paying taxes, reducing this once noble monument to a lonely ruin, overlooking the North Sea. Fortunately, the Aberdeenshire Council has taken a renewed interest in the historic landmark. In October 2007, public access to the castle was discontinued so that restoration construction could begin to convert the old castle into holiday apartments.

With the Duke of Clarence now being very likely to ascend the Throne, the Earl of Erroll found it quite convenient to be married to his daughter. He was able to use this position to be appointed a Lord of the Bedchamber to King George IV and later Master of the Horse to Queen Adelaide. Upon William IV's ascension, the Earl was also given a knighthood in the Royal Guelphic Order, more commonly called the Royal Hanoverian Order, followed a few years later by the Order of the Thistle, the highest chivalric order in Scotland.

In 1834, the Earl was given the additional title of Baron Kilmarnock. This title referred to a second Earldom the Hays family enjoyed prior to joining in the Jacobite rebellion against King George II in 1746, resulting in a forfeiture of the titles. The current creation is in the peerage of the United Kingdom, whereas the other titles held by the Earl of Erroll are created in the peerage of Scotland. The result being these two sets of titles having different succession rules. Titles created in the United Kingdom generally follow the rule of Salic law, meaning they can only be inherited by the male line descendants of the person for whom the title was created. However, Scottish titles typically allowed for female succession if a peer died without sons but had surviving daughters. This leads to the possibility of the titles separating and being inherited by different people, an event that would take place in 1941.

William and Elizabeth had four children: Ida, William, Agnes, and Alice. Ida would marry the Earl of Gainsborough and become the ancestress to the bulk of William IV's living descendants today. Agnes married the Earl Fife and her descendants will bring this line of illegitimate royal descendants to marry members of the legitimate royal family. Conversely, Alice remained childless but made an interesting marriage, nonetheless.

Lady Alice Hay married in 1874 to Charles Allen, a charlatan who, with much of his family, claimed to be a male line descendant of the Stuart Kings of England and Scotland. The story, as they told it, was that that Charles's father and uncle, named Charles and John respectively were the grandsons of Prince Charles Stuart, generally known to history as the "Young Pretender," himself being a grandson of King James II.

The brothers, John and Charles, concocted the whole tale after the death of their father, one Thomas Allen, a naval officer from Wales. They contended that Thomas was a child of Prince Charles and his wife, Luise of Stolberg, and that he had been hidden fearing reprisals from the last Jacobite Rebellion. The story is completely without foundation, but that does not prevent this dubious duo of brothers from styling themselves Count of Albany. Actually they used the more romantic French spelling, Count d'Albanie, based on the alias that Prince Charles used throughout his later life in exile. Luckily the Charles "Stuart" who married Lady Agnes Hay was the last of this suspicious line so their pretentions died with him when he left the earth childless in 1880.

The 18th Earl of Erroll was succeeded by his only son, also named William, in 1846. He spent much of his life tending to Slains Castle and the Cruden Bay area. He sometimes worked with an architect also named William Hays, a distant cousin. Around the time he inherited the castle and the title, he organized a small fishing village into a functional port which was named for him, Port Erroll. Shortly after, he joined the Rifle Guards, seeing action in the Crimean War and being wounded at the Battle of Alma.

In the early days of his military career, he was stationed in Canada where he met his wife, Eliza Gore, a granddaughter of the 2nd Earl of Arran. William and Eliza mostly retired to their Castle on the North Sea after his military career, entertaining the celebrities of the day during the later part of summer when it was desirable to not be in muggy London. Although he was not a guest at the Castle, it did capture the attention of a struggling novelist named Bram Stoker during a visit to the area. He documented that Slains inspired his descriptions of Castle Dracula is his most famous novel.

Although William and Eliza would have seven children, two would tragically die in their infancy, one being the heir-apparent, if only for two days. Of the five surviving children, the two daughters, Cecilia and Florence would each marry, but neither had children. The two younger sons, Arthur and Francis, would not even marry. Arthur lived a military life, serving as a Gentleman Usher to three monarchs, Victoria, Edward VII and George V. Francis travelled the world, but committed suicide in Australia at the age of 34.

This leaves Charles, who succeeded as the 20th Earl of Erroll in 1891. He spent much of his early life in the military, retiring from active duty in 1900 and being granted a knighthood in the Order of the Thistle the following year. Now home from the service, he concentrated on his duties as a member of the House of Lords, serving as Lord-in-Waiting (the title given the government Whip) during the administration of Arthur Balfour. He returned to active duty as a Brigadier General during the First World War.

Charles had married in 1875 to Mary L'Estrange, a descendant of the Earls of Scarborough. They had three sons, Victor, Serald, and Ivan, the younger two also seeing action during World War I. Serald would not leave children, and Ivan's descendants are via two of his three daughters, the Gurneys and Dares of London.

Victor's life was fully lived prior to becoming an Earl as he only outlived his father by seven months. He had entered the Diplomatic Services in 1900, serving the next 20 years as various under-secretaries. During the Great War, he was stationed in Denmark as a first Secretary, which was followed up by becoming the British Chargés d'Affaires in Berlin when diplomatic ties were restored following the War until a new Ambassador could arrive. He remained in Berlin as a Councilor until 1921, moving on to the commission which oversaw the occupation of the Rhineland.

Lord Kilmarnock, as he was known most of his life, also was an aspiring writer. His only novel to get published, *Ferelith*, came out in 1903. He later wrote two plays in the 1920's.

Upon entering the Diplomatic Service, Victor married Lucy Mackenzie, daughter of a Scottish Baronet, and promptly had three children, two sons and a daughter. The daughter, Rosemary, met and married an army officer during the time her father served on the Rhineland Commission, Lt. Col. Rupert Ryan. Born in Australia but educated in Britain, Ryan would replace his father-in-law on the Commission after the latter's death in 1928 and serve until the end of the occupation.

Retiring from the military, he became a salesman for an arms manufacturing firm assigned to territory throughout southeast Asia. After leaving this position and divorcing Rosemary, all within a year, he returned to his native Australia to oversee a large ranch he had inherited from his parents, taking his and Rosemary's only child, Patrick, with him. Rupert would go on to serve in World War II, then in the Australian House of Representatives. Today Rupert and Rosemary's descendants continue to live in Australia. Their son, Patrick passed away in 1989 leaving a son and daughter.

Victor and Lucy's elder son would become the subject of books and movies. Well, at least his death would. Josslyn Hay lived want many might call a squandered life. Born into the one of the most ancient noble families of Scotland, in

1901, young Hay had no trouble getting into Eton. But he did have trouble staying there, being dismissed after two years of letting a lascivious lifestyle get in the way of his studies. In an effort to keep some control of his wayward son, his father took him with him to Berlin and put him to work as an honorary attaché. However, when Lord Kilmarnock was appointed High Commissioner in the Rhineland, young Josslyn remained in Berlin to serve under the new Ambassador, Viscount D'Abernon.

In 1922, Josslyn returned to London, ostensibly to take the necessary test to enter full diplomatic service. However, he quickly took up with Lady Edina Gordon, a married woman with one divorce already under her belt. Being the daughter of the 8th Earl de la Warr, Edina was born into the same society as Josslyn, but also shared his taste for sexual adventures. She quickly dumped poor Mr. Gordon and married Josslyn, eight years her junior, in September 1923, her third of what would eventually become five marriages.

British society had come quite a ways in the past twenty years, but not far enough to accept Josslyn and Edina's unconventional marriage and even more unconventional lifestyle. So they escaped the notoriety by moving to Kenya, financed with Edina's money. In Kenya, they settled among several other expatriates in an area outside Nairobi known as Happy Valley. These young, wealthy settlers were notorious for their hedonistic lifestyles. Alcohol and drugs flowed freely, sexual inhibitions thrown to the wind. However, to play in these games, one had to have money and Josslyn did not have his own. The Hay family fortunes were no longer what they had been in their heyday and by now the family estate, Slains Castle had even been sold. Josslyn's debts were rising and he started stealing from his wife to cover them.

Edina discovered she was being swindled and returned to London to obtain a divorce in early 1930. As soon as he received word he divorce was final, Josslyn remarried Molly Ramsay-Hill, another former wife of two other men. Molly quickly fell in with the debauchery of the Happy Valley set, but it consumed her. She died of a drug overdose in 1939.

The widowed Josslyn Hay, now 21st Earl of Erroll, remained in Kenya carrying on affairs with one married lady after another, and sometimes not after. This wanton behavior caught up to him in 1941 when his body was discovered in his car on the side of the road with a bullet in his head.

The murder investigation captured the imagination of a world gripped by war. As more and more details about the Earl's lifestyle became known, the list of suspects became longer and longer. The murder became the subject of a bestselling book, *White Mischief*, and a movie by the same name. It is now known that the culprit was the man who was tried and acquitted of the murder, Sir "Jock" Broughton, a Baronet whose much younger wife was one of Erroll's many lovers. Lack of evidence at the time prompted the acquittal but guilt still persecuted the killer, leading to his suicide a year later.

When the 40-year-old Earl was murdered, his titles were divided. His only child, Diana, who was raised by her mother, Edina, in England, inherited his Scottish titles becoming the Countess of Erroll and Lady Hay. The Barony of Kilmarnock did not allow female succession so it passed to Josslyn's younger brother, Gilbert.

The Countess of Erroll was among the dozen peeresses to take their seats in the House of Lords in 1963 when the law was changed to allow women admittance. Prior to this peeresses *suo jure*, the term for peeresses in their own right, were typically considered place holders until the title passed to on to their son or other male relative. In older days, husbands of such ladies shared the title and were usually treated at the peer instead of their wife. Today, succession to a title by a lady is rather uncommon, but at least when they get there, they are treated with a little more equality than their ancestresses.

In 1946, Diana married Iain Moncreiffe, who would eventually succeed as the Chief of his Clan and the baronetcy that accompanied it. Iain had served in World War II in the Scots Guards, afterwards being made an attaché in Moscow. His true love was genealogy and he authored or co-authored several works relating to Georgian and Byzantine nobility as well as Scottish heraldry. After his brief diplomatic career, he served several positions under the Lyon King of Arms, the senior heraldic official of Scotland. He eventually became a barrister specializing in heraldic and inheritance issues. Iain and Diana had three sons before divorcing in 1964. Although he remarried, Iain had no further children.

After the divorce, Diana also remarried, to Raymond Carnegie, a grandson of the 7th Earl of Southesk and cousin to the 11th Earl who married Princess Maud of Fife, also a William IV descendant. Diana and Raymond had one more child, Jocelyn, who lives today with his wife and children in France.

Of the three sons of the Countess's first marriage, the eldest, Merlin, followed his mother as Earl after her death in 1978, keeping the Hay family name. His siblings would carry their father's name, Moncreiffe. Today the 24th Earl is an acknowledged expert in information technology and maintains his seat as his wife's ancestral home, Woodbury Hall in Bedfordshire. He is the father of four twenty-something children.

Diana's younger son, Peregrine Moncreiffe succeeded his father as the Chief of the Clan in 1985, confirmed by the Lord Lyon King of Arms in 2001. As the Earldom of Erroll is historically closely tied to the Hay family it was determined the Moncreiffes would be represented by the line of the 2nd son. Peregrine and his family make their home at the Moncreiffe family seat in Perthshire.

Diana's only daughter, Alexandra, had a relationship with Michael Wigan, later the 6th Baronet, in the later 1970's producing a son Ivar. She later married Jocelyn Connell and has two more daughters. Although Ivar is Sir Michael's only son, he is ineligible to inherit the baronetcy since his parents never married.

When Josslyn, Earl of Erroll was murdered in 1941, his title, Baron Kilmarnock, went to his younger brother, Gilbert. He adopted the name Boyd, the ancestral name associated with his paternal ancestry, the Earls of Kilmarnock, a title that was forfeited in 1745 when the 4th Earl joined in rebellion against King George II. The family name had been changed to Hay in 1758 with the inheritance of the Earldom of Erroll.

Gilbert, now the 6th Baron Kilmarnock, had married Rosemary, a daughter of Viscount Wimborne in 1926, with whom he had six children, although a set of twin girls were both dead within 48 hours of their birth. Gilbert and Rosemary divorced in 1955 and Gilbert remarried the same year to Denise Coker. She would give him two more children. Gilbert died in 1975 and was succeeded by his eldest son, Alastair.

Alastair Boyd was born in 1927 and had a standard upbringing of the titled class with only an upper-middle class income. He went to King's College in Cambridge and served a stint in the Irish Guards in the late 1940's. After his parents' divorce in 1955, he moved to the Andalusia region, in southern Spain, to the town of Ronda which he had discovered on a trip two years earlier. We would remain in Spain for the next 20 years with the wife he married shortly before the move, Diana Gibson. Ultimately the marriage ended, childless, with Diana returning to England.

While in Spain, Alastair founded a language school and began his own career as a writer. He wrote several books about his adopted country, a few are travel guides which continue to be updated. Alastair found love again with the mother of one of his language school students, Mrs. Hilary Bailey, known as Hilly.

Hilly Bailey's first husband had been novelist Kingsley Amis, who was the father of her children. In his last years of life, becoming something of a cantankerous old man, Amis lived with Alastair and Hilly. When Hilly became pregnant with Alastair's only child, James, known by his Spanish name, Jaime, she was still legally married to Shackleton Bailey. He dragged his feet through the divorce proceedings causing Jaime to be born prior to his parents' marriage and making him ineligible to inherit the Barony of Kilmarnock.

After becoming Baron in 1975, Alastair returned to England, serving actively in the House of Lords until so-called reform measures removed most hereditary Peers from that body. He embraced the Social Democrats Party and nurtured the careers of up and coming politicians through the party.

When being a hereditary peer no longer had meaning in the House of Lords following passage of the House of Lords Act of 1999, Kilmarnock and his wife returned to their beloved Andalusia where died in 2009, followed by Hilly a year later. Since Jaime was ineligible to succeed due to being born prior to his parents' marriage, the Barony passed to Alastair's next younger brother, Robin, who is known as "Tiger." The future succession seems secure as Tiger Kilmarnock has two sons, the eldest of whom, Simon, is also father to a son, Lucien, born in 2007.

The remainder, and majority, of the large number of descendants of Lady Elizabeth FitzClarence and the 18th Earl of Erroll come through their daughters, Ida, Countess of Gainsborough and Agnes, Countess of Fife, and will be examined over the next three chapters.

Chapter 6: The Noels

Lady Ida Hay was the eldest daughter of the 18th Earl of Erroll and, through her mother, granddaughter of King William IV and his long-time paramour, the actress Mrs. Jordan. She married, in 1841, Charles Noel, later the 2nd Earl of Gainsborough.

The Gainsborough title and Noel name both have a bit of a convoluted history. These Earls were of a second creation of the title, the first having been created for one Edward Noel in 1682. In due course of time, the first creation became extinct with the death of the 6th Earl in 1798. The sister of this last Earl, Lady Jane Noel, married Gerard Edwardes, himself an illegitimate grandson of the 4th Duke of Hamilton.

Jane and Gerard's son, also named Gerard, adopted his mother's maiden name of Noel in 1798 and married Diana, Baroness Barham in her own right. Through a special remainder created for his father-in-law, Gerard Noel also inherited a baronetcy, which was, in turn, passed to his and Diana's son, Charles, who was created Earl of Gainsborough, and became the father of Lady Ida Hay's husband.

In an interesting genealogical twist, had the parents of Gerard Edwardes been married, as has been proposed by some historians but lacking in proof, the present day Earls of Gainsborough would also be the Dukes of Hamilton. The senior line of the Hamiltons became extinct in 1895 at which time the descendants of the peculiarly named Lord Anne Hamilton, Gerard Edwardes' father, inherited the Dukedom. If Lord Anne and Mary Edwardes had indeed married, Gerard would be the eldest legitimate son and his descendant, the 3rd Earl of Gainsborough would have succeeded as Duke in 1895.

However, no proof has been found of a marriage between Lord Anne and Mary Edwardes so their son continues to be determined as illegitimate. Therefore the Dukedom passed to the descendants of a later, proven marriage for Lord Anne instead.

The Earl of Gainsborough and his wife converted to Catholicism in 1851, an act that generally kept the family at arm's length from the then Queen Victoria - at least at further length than her other cousins descended from her "Uncle King." Previously, Lady Ida had been quite close to the Queen and was even one of her bridesmaids at her wedding to Prince Albert.

Charles and Ida had five children: Blanche, Constance, Charles, Edith and Edward. Blanche married an organist and lived quietly, dying without children in 1881. Edith entered the Church as a nun. The remaining three children have plenty of descendants to make up for the two who do not.

Lady Constance Noel married Sir Henry Bellingham, 4th Baronet, in 1874. The title Baronet was created for Henry's great-grandfather, Sir William, a naval commissioner. Sir William's claim in history is his close involvement with outfitting the exploration team of George Vancouver. for whom the Canadian city is named. Appropriately enough, a bay near Vancouver is now named for Bellingham, as is a town in the U.S.A.'s state of Washington - All of this despite the fact that Bellingham never even saw the Pacific Ocean.

The Bellinghams were an Irish family from county Louth. Sir Henry pursued a career in public service. He served Louth in the British Parliament in the 1880s followed up by serving as High Sheriff and later Lord Lieutenant back in his home county. In addition to serving his homeland, he served his Pope as Private Chamberlain, - actually three Popes: Pius IX, Leo XII, and Pius X.

Of Henry and Constance's four children, the elder daughter became a nun as Sister (later Mother) Mary Emanuel, and the younger daughter, the Marchioness of Bute. The Crichton-Stuarts of Bute will be discussed in the next chapter.

The elder son, Edward, succeeded his father as Baronet, in 1921, as well as Lord Lieutenant of county Louth, a title he would hold only a year until Irish independence. He lived most of his life as a soldier serving in the Boer Wars, and both World Wars. He briefly served in the Seanad Éireann, the first upper house in Ireland's parliament, between the wars. Late in life he also served as Vice-Consul in the British embassy in Guatemala.

In 1904, Edward married a widow, Mrs. Charlotte Gough and with her had an only daughter, Charlotte. Charlotte married Ronald Hawker, a descendant of Dorothy Jordan's daughter Lucy Ford. Charlotte's only son is now elderly and unmarried.

Sir Edward was the last of the Baronets to live in Castle Bellingham in county Louth. He sold the 17th century castle to the Irish State which, in turn, sold it to one Dermot Meehan who developed it into a hotel, which is how it remains today.

Since Edward only had a daughter, his baronetcy passed to the son of his younger brother, Roger, who is also named Roger. Sir Roger made his home in Cheshire, in western England. There he raised his two sons who would each become Baronet. The elder, Sir Noel, died childless in 1999. The younger, Sir Anthony, is the present Baronet and currently lives in Thailand. His only child is his heir, William. In his late teens, William now makes his home in California near his mother, where he has fallen in with the children of some of Hollywood's biggest names.

In 1881, the Earldom of Gainsborough passed to Charles Noel, elder son of the 2nd Earl and Lady Ida Hay. Charles was born and died at Campden House in Chipping Campden, Gloucestershire. Campden House is a rebuilt mansion, the original manor house being burnt during the Civil War, and served as home to the Earls of Gainsborough in the 19th Century. More recently they have tended toward their principal estate at Exton Park, Rutland.

Charles, while still heir to his father and thus styled Viscount Campden, married firstly to Augusta Berkeley, a maternal granddaughter of the Irish Earl of Kenmare. She died in 1877, four years before she could become Countess of Gainsborough. Her only child, Agnes, died unmarried in1915. It is Charles' second wife who became Countess and ancestress of the subsequent Earls. She was Mary-Elizabeth Dease, a descendant of King Charles II through her mother, Charlotte Jerningham. Charles and Mary-Elizabeth would have five more children, three sons and two daughters.

The eldest son, Arthur, succeeded to the Earldom in 1926. His 1915 marriage to Alice Eyre produced three children: Maureen, later Baroness Dormer, Anthony, the 5th Earl, and Gerard. Prior to becoming Earl, Arthur, as well as both of his brothers, saw action in the First World War, the youngest brother, Robert, dying in Africa from disease contracted while on active duty. Arthur would be the Earl of Gainsborough for only eight months as he died in 1927.

Arthur was succeeded by his elder son, Anthony. Described in his obituary as the largest landowner in England's smallest county, Rutland, the 5th Earl of Gainsborough was an adamant defender of rural self-government. Serving on several boards and commissions, not to mention in the House of Lords, he opposed dictates from London about how resources of the rural area should be managed. He fought against the absorption of Rutland by Leicestershire, which happened in 1974, professing it would never work. He lived long enough to be proven right and saw the 1997 re-establishment of the Rutland County Council, a body on which he once served.

Married in 1947 to Mary Stourton, granddaughter of the 25th Baron Stourton, Anthony sired a large brood of a family with eight children, evenly divided between sons and daughters Sadly, one daughter died in infancy. His descendants include not only the current Earl and his son and heir, but also Viscount Flojambe, heir to the Earl of Liverpool.

Anthony's brother, the Hon. Gerard Noel, also has a connection to the Royal Family among his family, albeit somewhat roundabout. His daughter, Elizabeth is married to the step-son of Andrew Parker-Bowles, first husband to Her Royal Highness the Duchess of Cornwall.

The 4th Earl of Gainsborough's sister, Lady Norah, married into another prominent titled family of Britain, the Bentincks. This family is actually a foreign import as they came to Britain with the Glorious Revolution that brought

William and Mary to the Throne in 1689. Count Hans Willem Bentinck was a chief advisor to Willem, Prince of Orange, and came with him to Britain when Willem became King William III to sit alongside his wife Queen Mary II. There are long standing rumors that Bentinck may have been not only an advisor, but also a lover to the new King. His descendant, the current Earl of Portland, has a novel way of refuting this; he claims Count Bentinck was just too dull to be gay.

Whatever Count Bentinck's orientation, he was married and produced heirs. Bentinck himself was created Earl of Portland and his eldest son was later elevated to Duke. The Dukes of Portland continued over the centuries but became extinct in 1990. Since the Earldom had been created for a previous generation of the family, it was able to pass to the younger sons of Count Bentinck, which brings us to one Robert Bentinck, who married Lady Norah Noel. In addition to any British titles they may inherit, this family also has the right, by special permission of Queen Victoria, to continue to use their countly title from the Holy Roman Empire. So Robert was styled Count Robert Bentinck.

Count and Countess Bentinck had two children, Brydgytte and Henry. Brydgytte returned to the land of her ancestors when she married Dutch nobleman Adriaan van der Wyck. Adriaan carried the title Jonkheer, a title which does not have an accurate translation into English. Perhaps saying the Noble Adriaan van der Wyck would be the best way to capture the sense of the meaning. Adriaan and Brydgytte's five children and their descendants have remained in the Netherlands.

Count Henry ultimately inherited the Earldom of Portland upon the extinction of the ducal line in 1990. Henry, who discontinued using the title Count, was the first to break from the traditions of European aristocracy and entered the regular workforce. He is best known as a producer of television commercials and for the BBC, but he also did a stint as a farm hand in Tasmania. It should therefore not be surprising that neither of his marriages were with members of the titled elite. Henry had the title Earl for only seven years before his own death in 1997.

Being raised by a television producer, it is no wonder that his only son and heir, Timothy, entered a similar field: acting. Tim Bentinck, as he is known professionally, was born during his father's time in Tasmania. After a somewhat aimless start, he has found a successful career in both voice-over and stage performances. A thoroughly down-to-earth fellow, he prefers Tim to "your Lordship." Married since 1979, he is the father of two twenty-something boys, William and Jasper, who he describes on his website as being a major intellect (William) and a future rock deity (Jasper).

Tim Bentinck's two elder sisters are also occupied with their own families, the elder, Sorrel, being formerly married to the Lister-Kaye Baronet and the younger, Anna to a couple of fellows before starting a family without a husband. The Bentinck siblings have done many things during their lives and been many people. They have also known tragedy, as Anna lost a set of twins within minutes of their birth.

Several of the families that have married into the descendants of King William and Mrs. Jordan have belonged to the Peerage, that is, the titled nobility of the British Isles, but others have belonged to what is known as the Landed Gentry, a series of families that, though not noble, have long family histories typically associated with a particular place or estate. A classic example of such a family is the Steuart Fothringhams, Lairds of Murthly, in Perthshire.

Laird is an ancient Scottish designation that is derived from "Lord of the Manor," and has come to be used to differentiate between these types of lords and the noble title "Lord" which has been ranked at the same level as an English

Baron. Thus it is as the owners and caretakers of the Estate of Murthly that the Steuart Fothringhams can be termed as Lairds.

Carola Noel, granddaughter of the 3rd Earl of Gainsborough, brought this landed family into the fold of William IV descendants by marrying Thomas Steuart Fothringham in 1936. The Murthly estate is famous for its beautifully maintained international woods, comprised mostly of conifers such as Douglas firs brought to Scotland from the United States in the early 1800s, Serbian spruce, Chilean pine, and varieties of hemlock. There continue to be additions made and a more diverse choice of trees planted.

The Steuart Fothringhams, like the trees they care for, are on the brink of becoming a very large family. Carola and Thomas had only three children, but they multiplied into nine grandchildren who are now the parents of a growing army of great-grandchildren.

Chapter 7: The Crichton-Stuarts

The 1905 marriage of Augusta Bellingham to John Crichton-Stuart, 4th Marquess of Bute, marked the joining of a descendant of the newer Germanic Hanover/Saxe-Coburg dynasty of British Kings with a descendant of the old regime of the Stuart Kings of Scotland.

The Crichton-Stuarts, named only Stuart until 1805, are direct male line descendants of King Robert II of Scotland (died 1390), the first of the Stuart Kings, through his illegitimate son, John, the Black Stewart, so named because of his dark complexion.

Over the centuries, the Stuarts picked up several titles, beginning with a baronetcy in 1627. This was followed by the Earldom of Bute, with its subsidiary viscountcy and three lordships, in 1703. The first title in the Peerage of Great Britain, the previous ones all being in that of Scotland, was given to the 3rd Earl's wife as Baroness Mount Stuart, a title that merged with the others when their son succeeded both of his parents. In addition to his own inheritance, he married the heiress of vast Welsh lands and in recognition of this was created in Baron Cardiff in 1776. This Lord Bute was further titled Earl of Windsor and Viscount Mountjoy, revivals of titles held by his wife's family, and Marquess of Bute in 1796. His grandson, the 2nd Marquess, also succeeded his maternal grandfather as the 7th Earl of Dumfries, Viscount Ayr and 15th Lord Crichton. The current Marquess carries this lengthy list of titles to this day.

Of the more notable ancestors, none are more so than the 3rd Earl of Bute, Prime Minster of Great Britain 1762-1763, the first Scot to hold the position after the Act of Union of 1707, which created Great Britain. Though a brief term, it was at a momentous one, seeing the end of the Seven Years' War, alternately known outside Britain as the French and Indian War, the 3rd Silesian War, or the Pomeranian War.

The title Marquess itself is an interesting story. The titles of the British Peerage system typically have their roots in foreign languages. For example, Duke comes from the

Latin dux. Earl is the only one that is uniquely British, being derived from an ancient Celtic term. The term Marquess came to Britain with the conquering Normans in 1066 and is an attempt to anglicize the French title Marquis. This title has recognizable variations in other languages such as Marqués or Marchese. Many try to tie the word also to the German Markgraf, but this term seems to have a different origination. In present-day Britain, with worldwide media available 24 hours a day, the term Marquess has become nearly interchangeable with Marquis in day-to-day usage.

It is with all of this history and all of these titles that the 4th Marquess, or Marquis, traditionally named John Crichton-Stuart, married Augusta Bellingham, direct matrilineal descendant of Mrs. Jordan and her royal lover, the Duke of Clarence, later King William IV. By this point, not only had the Marquess acquired many titles, but also had amassed extremely large tracts of property, becoming the largest land owner in the British Isles.

John also held an interest in Morocco and bought several acres there as well, founded a hotel in Tangier, and became proprietor of an English-language newspaper, *The Tangier Gazette*. In the 1930s he oversaw the sale of much of his Welsh land holdings, the unparalleled sale causing quite the media sensation just as much the world was working its way out of a Depression and into a World War.

John and Augusta, who was herself honored as a Dame of the British Empire in 1918, had seven children, five of them boys. Through their eldest daughter, Lady Mary, the Crichton-Stuarts are now connected to European nobility. Mary's elder daughter, Ione, married Baron Christian von Oppenheim and made their home in Spain. The younger daughter, Lady Jean, married a son of the 7th Earl of Abington, the Hon. James Bertie. James and Jean had two sons, the elder of whom became the Grand Master of the Sovereign Military Order of Malta, the first Brit to do so since 1258.

The eldest Crichton-Stuart brother, of course named John, succeeded his father as 5th Marquess of Bute in 1947. After serving in the Royal Navy during World War II, he made his mark in the world of ornithology. He purchased the islands of St. Kilda as a means of preserving the delicate ecosystems there. He then gifted the islands to the National Trust for Scotland so they could be properly maintained for future generations. He also gifted his remaining Welsh property, Cardiff Castle, to the City of Cardiff. Today the

Castle houses museums and, sitting in luscious Bute Park, is used as a concert venue.

The 5th Marquess married Lady Eileen Forbes, daughter of the 8th Earl of Granard, in 1932. They had four children, three sons and a daughter. The daughter, Lady Fiona, and her husband, Michael Lowsley-Williams, moved to Spain, making their living there in real estate with their four sons. The three sons remained in Britain and their descendants make up the core of the Crichton-Stuart family today.

The eldest son, - yes, he too is named John, - succeeded to the Marquessate in 1956. Dedicated to historic preservation, the 6th Marquess sat on several boards, most notably the National Trust for Scotland, serving as its chair. He began an ambitious restoration of his home estate, Mount Stuart, in the late 1980s, work that has continued under his son, the current Marquess.

Johnny Dumfries, as the 7th and current Marquess was known during his father's lifetime, was a professional race car driver, winning several formula races, crowning his achievements with a win at Le Mans in 1988. Since the death of his father, in 1993, he still prefers to be called Johnny, but now it is Johnny Bute.

A very modern individual, Johnny Bute places less emphasis on his title and more on what he can do for Scotland and the rather large corner of it that he owns. Continuing the restorative work begun by his father, Johnny has proven his dedication to the land he owns and preserving its heritage for future generations.

Over the course of two marriages, Johnny is now the father of four children: three girls and a boy who is now styled Earl of Dumfries. In a nod to the conventional from an unconventional Marquess, the boy is also named John.

Of the several living Crichton-Stuart cousins descended from the 4th Marquess and Augusta Bellingham, one of the more notable is their grandson, Frederik Crichton-Stuart. He is the son of Lord Rhidian, Augusta's youngest son, and Selina Gerthe van Wijk, herself the daughter of a Dutch diplomat.

Freddy, as he is universally known, followed a similar path as his cousin, Andrew Bertie, becoming heavily involved with the Sovereign Military Order of Malta, known colloquially as the Order of St. John. In 2008, when Bertie died, he was succeeded as the Grand Master by Matthew Festing, until then Grand Prior of England. In the position of

Grand Prior, Festing has been succeeded by Freddy Crichton-Stuart.

His installation as Grand Prior completes a circle begun when his ancestors staunchly supported Mary, Queen of Scots, until her execution was ordered by her cousin, Queen Elizabeth I of England. One of Elizabeth's acts to end the religious war in England in favor of a protestant Church of England was to dismember the Priory. It lay in abeyance for the next fours and a half centuries until Elizabeth's namesake, Elizabeth II, restored the Grand Priory in 1993. And now another Stuart is its Grand Prior.

Chapter 8: The Duffs

Lady Agnes Hay (I1829-1869) married, in 1846 in Paris, James Duff, who after 1857, was the 5th Earl of Fife. Life with the Earl was nearly the opposite of life with her parents. The Errolls had been a very social family and always a presence at Court. The Earl was a notorious recluse, who wandered from his home, "Duff House," near Banff, only when he could otherwise not get out of doing so. This staying at home business did have one happy side affect: children, of whom they had five.

The eldest Duff daughter was Anne, born in 1847. She married the future 5th Marquess of Townshend. Like many Lords-in-waiting, John Townshend served first in the House of Commons, having been elected from Tamworth in

Staffordshire. His term was from 1856 to 1863, when he succeed his father as Marquess. John and Anne Townshend had two children, John and Agnes.

John, the 6th Marquess of Townshend after 1899, married in 1905 Gwladys Sutherst, who became one of the earliest ladies to be what we now would call a screenwriter. She was also a playwright and novelist and was associated with the Claredon Film Company early in its existence.

Gwladys Townshend also became known for a more "spirited" matter. She is one of the many occupants of Raynham Hall, seat of the Marquesses of Townshend, to have encountered, and discussed at length, its celebrated ghost, the Brown Lady. The spirit is so named because she reportedly appears as a brown haze, lacking real definition, but seeming like a lady in dresses and a veil. She is believed to be the ghost of Audrey, Viscountess Townshend, mother of the 1st Marquess. The story goes that after being discovered of infidelity, she was kept prisoner in Raynham Hall and never allowed to see her children again. Whatever the story, a photograph of the Brown Lady taken in 1936 is considered one of the best "ghost pictures" ever taken.

Like his own parents, John & Gwladys also had only two children, one son and one daughter. The son, the 7th

Marquess of Townshend, has the distinction of being the longest serving member of the British Peerage. On March 2nd, 2009 he broke the record, and at the time of his death thirteen months later, at age 93, he had been a Peer for 88 years, 5 months and 10 days. Like his mother, he was in the theater arts, serving as Chairman of Anglia Television for three decades until his retirement in 1986. This Marquess was married three times, first to Elizabeth Luby (later Lady Galt, wife of Sir James), then to Ann Darlow, who died in 1988, and finally to Philippa Montgomerie, who was the widow of Humphrey Swire. By his first two wives, he became the father of five children: Carolyn, Joanna and Charles by Elizabeth, and John and Katherine by Ann.

Lady Carolyn Townshend, the name she continues to be known by after two failed marriages, is a London event and party planning socialite who married two wealthy business men. First, she married Goodyear executive Antonio Capellini, and then briefly to Seagram's CEO, Edgar Bronfman Sr. She has one grown son by Capellini who is now married with a family of his own.

Lady Joanna, who also has retained her maiden name, is now on her third marriage, this one to Christian Boegner.

She also has one grown son, Francis, by her first husband, Jeremy Bradford.

Charles, now the 8th Marquess, was the elder son and heir to his father. He is very involved with the local community surrounding Raynham Hall. One notable example is his devotion to renovations was adding new bells to the Church of East Raynham, whose renovation caught the interest of even the Queen, prompting a 2002 royal visit during the construction. While still Lord Raynham, his first wife, Hermione Ponsonby, sadly was killed in a car crash in 1985. Charles remarried five years later to Mrs. Alison Marshall. Lord Townshend has two grown children by his first wife, including heir, Thomas.

The 7th Marquess's younger children, John and Katherine have each married twice and have young children still at home. Katherine's first husband, Piers Dent has made a name for himself as an aerial photographer. Lord Townshend's lone sister, Lady Elizabeth, married a Baronet named Richard White and had one child, the current holder of that Baronetcy, Sir Christopher.

The only sibling of the 6th Marquess, Lady Agnes, married James Cunnighame-Durham, son of a diplomat by the same name. Their son, Nicholas was killed in World War

II, and their daughter, Victoria, died unmarried, aged 94, in 2002.

The Countess of Fife's second daughter, Ida, was born in 1848 at Duff House. Ida married twice, to Adrian Hope and William Wilson, and was divorced both times. With Adrian, she had three daughters: Agnes, Mildred, and Ethel. The eldest daughter, Agnes, married Edwin Phillips de Lisle, whose father, Ambrose, was a prominent layman of the Catholic Church. They had a large family of eight children, which today have turned into dozens of descendants. The second daughter, Mildred, remained unmarried.

The youngest daughter, Ethel, married John Lockhart-Mummery, a doctor of a Landed Gentry family. John became well-respected in the medical community and published works connecting heredity to likeliness to develop cancer. Ethel died childless, but John has descendants still living through his second marriage.

Lady Fife's only son, Alexander was born in 1849 in Edinburgh. It was through his father's friendship with the Prince of Wales (later Edward VII,) that he married Princess Louise, the Prince's eldest daughter. This marriage not only brought him into the British Royal Family, but also made him a brother-in-law to the future Queen of Norway, Louise's youngest sister, Maud. In preparation for marrying a royal princess, it was determined that being an Earl wasn't good enough so he was elevated to become the first Duke of Fife.

The Duke and the Princess had two surviving daughters, their only son being stillborn in 1890. When it became obvious there would be no more children, and Louise's father had finally succeeded his long-living mother, Queen Victoria, the creation of the Dukdom of Fife was reconstituted to allow the succession of the daughters and any male heirs they may have. The two girls, now teenagers, were also raised to the rank of Princess of Fife by their doting grandfather in 1905.

The elder daughter, Princess Alexandra, Duchess of Fife after 1912, married her first cousin, Prince Arthur, who was the only son and heir to the Duke of Connaught. As it happened, the old Duke outlived Arthur and that title passed to Arthur and Alexandra's only child, Alastair, who himself died unmarried in 1943 before he could also succeed as Duke of Fife.

The younger daughter, Princess Maud, married the Earl of Southesk and had one child, a son James, who today is the 3rd Duke of Fife, and has been since Princess Alexandra's death in 1959. James' mother had died in 1945, but his father lived on until 1992, dying at the age of 98. The current Duke, who now is also the Earl of Southesk, married Caroline, daughter of the 3rd Baron Forteviot in 1954, but divorced twelve years later. They have two grown children, David, styled Earl of Southesk by courtesy, and Lady Alexandra. Both are married with children, - Charles' three are in their teens, and Clare's only daughter is still in early primary school.

Lady Fife's third daughter, Agnes, was born in 1849. Agnes' marital adventures could be a book unto themselves. The short version is, at age 19, she eloped with Viscount Dupplin, the heir to the Earl of Kinnoull, and two years later had her first daughter, also named Agnes, but quickly grew tired of the boring Viscount. She eloped again in 1876, - losing her child to Dupplin in the process, - with Herbert Flower, whose brother, Cyril, was created Lord Battersea. This match suited her much better and they were truly happy together, according to family and friends, for the four years until Herbert died. Penniless and a social outcast, Agnes went to work in a hospital doing menial labor hoping to learn enough to become a nurse. While there, she met and was swept off her feet by a surgeon, Dr. Alfred Cooper, who became her third husband in 1882.

Alfred had a knack for being in the right place at the right time. It is how he met Agnes, and it is how he happened to be visiting friends in St. Petersburg, Russia at the same time as the then Duke of Edinburgh (2nd son of Queen Victoria) was marrying the Tsar's daughter. The Prince of Wales was also in attendance of the wedding and fell ill. Cooper was the first British doctor they could locate, so he cared for the ailing Prince, getting him back on his feet, and becoming friends at the same time. Edward did not forget this kindness shown him and awarded Alfred with a knighthood when he became King. One more tidbit about Alfred Cooper (later Sir Alfred): his medical specialty was venereal disease, and his clients were mostly the upper crust of society. Even though he must have had some truly sordid gossip to share, he never did.

Agnes, the daughter by Viscount Dupplin, married German diplomat Herbert von Hindenburg, a relative of the Imperial Field Marshal and later President of the German Republic. Their life was lived in relative obscurity, with one sadness being their only child, a daughter, who died at birth.

The eldest Cooper child was Stephanie, born in 1883. Her first marriage to stockbroker Arthur Levita brought financial security, which served her well after his death, in

1910, and also gave her the ability to take in her family members as needed during the lean years of the First World War. In the midst of the war, in 1916, Stephanie married Maurice Wingfield, known to his friends as Tolly. Stephanie had lovely daughters by Levita, Violet and Enid. Violet's line ended with the death of her only child, Nicholas Hirsch, in 1983. Enid married Euen Cameron and by him had an only son, Ian. Ian Cameron married Mary Mount, the daughter of a Baronet and by her has four children including the current Prime Minister, David Cameron.

The second Cooper daughter, Hermione (known as Mione to her family), married in 1904, at age 19, to Neil Arnott. The marriage was not a happy one but did produce one child, a son Ian. Ian died prematurely in 1950 and left a sole daughter, Portia. Portia ended her days in 2009 on the island of Cyprus, having been married to James Lord and leaving a son and a daughter as well as five grandchildren.

Agnes's fourth daughter, the third by Cooper, Sybil, came in 1886 and only lived to the age of 41. During that time she married Richard Hart-Davis of a landed family in Surrey. Sybil had two children, but it was believed by them that Richard was not their father. Sybil herself was always unsure of the paternity of her children, but Richard accepted them and raised them as his own. It is perhaps a blessing that Sybil's life was short, as it was tormented by mental illness which led her to living a religious-based life at the end in hopes of finding relief. But ultimately, she lost that battle, committing suicide.

The son, Rupert, born in 1907, went on to become a very well-known publisher, editor, author, and even briefly an actor. It is uncommon to come across his name without the term "Man of Letters" attached. In addition to his meticulous editing of hundreds of the letters of Oscar Wilde, he is also the author of a superb biography of Hugh Walpole, and published his own weekly correspondence with his old Eton professor, George Myttleton. Furthermore, he was an active member of the London Library and the Literary Society. In 1967, he was awarded a knighthood for his literary contributions.

Even though Rupert Hart-Davis spent a hectic schedule of dining with this group or attending that gala, he did not consider himself a social person. In one of his published letters he wrote:

> The fact that I am tolerably good at coping with
> people is misleading. I much prefer near-solitude,
> at any rate for long periods. Maybe too much of
> it would drive me back to the world of men, but

I've never had enough leisure to test the theory.[3]

This, "preference for solitude" did not include solitude from marriage. He did it four times; firstly and briefly to the actress Peggy Ashcroft; secondly to the mother of his three children, Comfort Borden-Turner; thirdly to Ruth Simon, whom he had loved for 17 years before marrying her and who died suddenly in his arms in a taxi; and fourthly to his former secretary, June Williams, who provided him companionship in his last years before dying at the age of 92.

Rupert's three children have made marks in the world in their own ways. The eldest, Bridget, married Baron Silsoe, and has lived the life of a political wife and mother of two. Duff, the elder of two sons, is himself a noted biographer and journalist, and the youngest, Adam, has also published several works, mostly on scientific or technical concerns, and like his father, has had a career so varied as to include television production and being an expert on toilets. Each of Rupert's children has married and each has two children of their own, with a new generation just starting to appear.

---

[3] Hart-Davis, Rupert. *The Lyttleton Hart-Davis Letters, Vol. III* (1981)

Sir Rupert's only sibling, Deirdre, also visited the altar four times. Her first husband, Ronald Balfour, the father of first two children, was killed in a car crash in 1941. The only thing worth remarking on her three subsequent marriages is that she had a third daughter by her third husband, Tony Bland.

The youngest of the Cooper kids, Duff, was the one to lead the most public life. After attending Eton he joined the foreign service, which spared him active duty in World War I until 1917 when he joined the Grenadier Guards. He received a DSO for his service. The most remarkable event of war life is that he survived it. He was the only one a tight knit group of friends from Eton to do so. This shared loss brought him closer to the only lady in the group, Lady Diana Manners, the "Lady Di" of her day. They married after the war, in 1919, and after much debate with the Diana's parents, the Duke and Duchess of Rutland. The Rutlands initially did not want the match. After all, Duff was not a Peer or even the son of one, but in the end Diana and Duff won out.

After the war, Duff returned to the foreign service, serving mostly in Egypt and Turkey. In 1924, he won a seat in Parliament from Oldham. He was a supporter of Baldwin, support which led to him losing his seat, along with many other Conservatives in 1929. He turned to literature while out of office and wrote a well-received biography of Talleyrand. With the threat of War once again looming on the Continent, he returned to government in the 1930s working his way up to First Lord of the Admiralty in 1937, only to resign a year later in protest of Neville Chamberlain's appeasement policies towards Hitler's Germany. He later served again, this time under Churchill, in minor roles during the war, eventually being the British liaison to the Free French and then Ambassador to Paris in 1944. He retired from public service in 1947, receiving a knighthood, and later a peerage as Viscount Norwich, and devoted the remaining seven years of his life to literature.

The Cooper-Manners marriage lasted 35 years but was wrought with infidelities. One such affair on Duff's side, in 1947, lead to the birth on an illegitimate son, William Patten, who only learned this truth after he was 50. William is a Unitarian pastor in Massachusetts. His mother was the quintessential political hostess, Susan Alsop. The story of this "long-lost" child became public only after the death of both biological parents involved. William recently wrote a memoir of his life, his relationship with his mother and the three men he called "father" at various times.

By Lady Diana, Cooper also fathered a son, the current Viscount Norwich. John Julius Norwich, as he is listed in television credits, has had a successful career as an author and in television. His areas of specialty are history and travel documentary, with a long list of productions he wrote and/or produced. Lord Norwich has been married twice and is the father of Artemis Cooper, who has followed in her father's footsteps as a historian, and of Jason Cooper, the heir to his title. Lord Norwich also has a daughter named Allegra by the late Enrica Huston, who, at the time, was the estranged wife of filmmaker, John Huston.

Lady Fife's youngest child, Alexina, born in 1851, is the one almost forgotten to history. She married a grandson of the Earl of Coventry, but died in 1882 at the young age of 31, leaving no children.

Chapter 9: The Kennedy-Erskines

Lady Augusta FitzClarence was only eight when her parents separated. Under the separation agreement between her father and mother, Augusta remained with her mother until she turned 13 and, at which time she went to live with her father. By the time she reached the height of her teen-aged years, Dora Jordan was dead and William had married Princess Adelheid of Saxe-Meiningen. Augusta and the younger half of her siblings found very close relationships with their step-mother. It was this soon-to-be Queen who facilitated most of the meetings of William's children with their spouses.

This was the case with Augusta when she met her future husband, John Kennedy, the younger son of the Earl of

Cassilis, who would later be elevated to the Marquessate of Ailsa. John's mother was Margaret Erskine, eventual heiress to the Lairdship Erskine of Dun, which was passed to her children. Since John's elder brother, Archibald, was heir to their father, the maternal Erskine inheritance fell to John. To reflect this inheritance, he changed his name to Kennedy-Erskine prior to his marriage to Augusta.

John and Augusta's marriage would only last not quite four years, as John died in 1831. However, the marriage did produce three children, William, Wilhelmina, and Millicent. Wilhelmina, the elder daughter would one day marry her cousin the 2nd Earl of Munster, but it is her childhood that she chose to write heavily about in a memoir published later in her life. It is through this memoir that we today can understand the lives of the children and grandchildren of King William during his later life.

While married to John, the family lived on the outskirts of London along the River Thames at an estate called Railshead next door to the estate of his parents. After his death, Augusta remained there until she remarried, an act ardently disapproved of by her in-laws. She was obliged to find a new home, so she turned to her father for help. Now

King, William was able to offer her and her family apartments in Kensington Palace.

Augusta's second marriage was to Lord John Gordon, a younger son of the 9th Marquess of Huntly. The Gordon family is one of the oldest and most distinguished families of Scotland. The Marquessate of Huntly is also the oldest Marquessate in Scotland, having been created in 1599. The 4th Marquess was further created Duke of Gordon and the two titles remained combined until the death of the 5th Duke and 8th Marquess in 1836. While the Dukedom then became extinct, the Marquessate passed to a more distant relative, Lord John's father. John and Augusta would not have any children.

Through Augusta's only son, William, named in honor of his royal grandfather, the Kennedy-Erskine name continued a couple more generations, but came extinct in 1980 with the death of Mrs. Millicent Lovett, the last child of William's only son, Augustus. Augustus's other children were twin boys, - one who died young and the other died childless, in 1963 - and a daughter, Violet.

Violet Kennedy-Erskine died most unusually, aged only 37. She was discovered dead in her room at the Empress Club in London on Christmas Day, 1934. The Coroner ruled she had committed suicide based on the fact that the room had been locked from the inside. However, she was discovered with her bed jacket wrapped around her throat and a dressing gown shoved into her mouth. It was an odd means for committing suicide. At the Coroner's Inquest, it was mentioned that the club's engineer entered through a window when it was discovered the door was locked and she was not responding to calls from the hall. Could someone have entered, or at least exited, that same way? Perhaps the Coroner was too quick to rule out foul play.

Violet had been named for her father's elder sister, Violet Erskine-Kennedy, who, by marriage, became Violet Jacob, the well known Scottish poet and author. This elder Violet married Arthur Jacob, and with him, had an only child, also named Arthur. The younger Arthur was still unmarried when he was killed in action in World War I, in Belgium.

The youngest child of Lady Augusta, Millicent Kennedy-Erskine, is the only one to have living descendants today. When Millicent married in 1855, she got to keep part of her name. Her husband was also a distant cousin, James Erskine-Wemyss. Just as her grandmother had been the heiress of the Erskines of Dun, James' mother was the heiress of the Erskines of Torriehouse. James' father was an heir in his own right to the Lairdship of Wemyss of Wemyss Castle. The names were joined by his parents' marriage to be Erskine-Wemyss.

Millicent and James had five children: Dora, Mary, Randolph, Hugo, and Rosslyn. Hugo died unmarried in 1933. Mary married Cecil Paget, a grandson of the 1st Marquess of Anglesey, and had three children, but they all died childless.

Dora married quite well in 1887 when she married the Lord Henry Grosvenor, son of the 1st Duke of Westminster, owner of extensive, and exclusive, properties throughout London. The title would eventually pass to their son, - but as he never married, - it would move onto a collateral branch of the family, where it remains today.

The youngest son was Rosslyn, who became a naval officer and eventually Admiral of the Fleet. His distinguished service in the Royal Navy through the First World War earned him a knighthood and, upon his retirement, a peerage as Baron Wester Wemyss. With his wife, Victoria Morier, daughter of noted diplomat, Sir Robert Morier, Rosslyn fathered only one child, a daughter, Alice. Therefore his Barony would expire upon his death in 1933.

The remaining Erskine-Wemyss, eldest son Randolph, would succeed his father in due course to the Lairdship of Wemyss of Castle Wemyss, was followed by his son, Michael, who ultimately succeeded to the headship of the entire clan of Wemyss. With this inheritance comes Wemyss Castle, a historically important building dating from 1421. Among its other historical events, it is the location where Mary, Queen of Scots, met her husband, Lord Darnley.

The Wemyss family today is headed by Michael's grandson and namesake, Michael Wemyss of that Ilk, whose maternal ancestry may be even more impressive, as his mother was from the Bruce family, this branch being the earls of Elgin and Kincardine. As Michael has only two grown daughters, the elder, as heiress, will presumably pass the name Wemyss on to any children she may have. The male line of the family will be continued by Michael's brother, Charles who has a son in his early twenties.

The Detailed Genealogy of the Descendants of King William IV

This genealogy attempts to list every descendant of King William IV, both legitimate and illegitimate. In any work of this nature there are bound to be errors and omissions. Corrections and additions are always welcome and shule be sent by email to daniel@danielawillis.com.

Symbols & Abbreviations:

*	Born
=	Married
+	Died
cr.	created
DBE	Dame of the Order of the British Empire
DCB	Dame Commander of the Order of the Bath
DCMG	Dame Commander of the Order of St. Michael and St. George
DCVO	Dame Commander of the Royal Victorian Order
dv.	Divorced
GBE	Knight Grand Cross of the Order of the British Empire
GCB	Knight Grand Cross of the Order of the Bath
GCH	Knight Grand Cross of the Order of Hanover
GCMG	Knight Grand Cross of the Order of St. Michael and St. George
GCVO	Knight Grand Cross of the Royal Victorian Order
HGDH	His/Her Grand Ducal Highness
HH	His/Her Highness
HIH	His/Her Imperial Highness
HI&RH	His/Her Imperial and Royal Highness
HM	His/Her Majesty
HRH	His/Her Royal Highness
HSH	His/Her Serene Highness
KCB	Knight Commander of the Order of the Bath
KCH	Knight Commander of the Order of Hanover
KCMG	Knight Commander of the Order of St. Michael and St. George
KCVO	Knight Commander of the Royal Victorian Order
KG	Knight of the Order of the Garter
KBE	Knight of the Order of the Britsh Empire
KH	Knight of the Order of Hanover
KP	Knight of the Order of St. Patrick
KT	Knight of the Order of the Thistle
Kt.	Knight Bachelor
ph.	posthumous
suc.	succeeded

HM William IV Henry**, King of the United Kingdom of Great Britain and Ireland, Elector of Hanover, Duke of Brunswick-Luneburg** (21 Aug 1765 London – 20 Jun 1837 Windsor) son of George III, King of the United Kingdom, etc.& Duchess Charlotte of Mecklenburg; cr. Duke of Clarence and St. Andrews, Earl of Munster 20 May 1789; suc. brother, George IV, as King, Elector, and Duke 26 Jun 1830
= 11 Jul 1818 London; **HSH Princess** Adelheid (**Adelaide**) Luise Therese Karoline Amelie **of Saxe-Meiningen**, Duchess of Saxony (13 Aug 1792 Meiningen – 2 Dec 1849 Middlesex) daughter of Georg I, Duke of Saxe-Meiningen Princess Luise Eleonore of Hohenlohe-Langenburg
issue by **Dorothy Bland** (known professionally as **Mrs. Jordan**) (22 Nov 1761 London – 5 Jul 1816 St. Cloud, France) daughter of Francis Bland & Catherine Mahoney:
Granted the style of children of a Marquess 24.5.1831:
I. **George** Augustus Frederick **FitzClarence, 1st Earl of Munster**, Viscount FitzClarence, Baron Tewkesbury (29 Jan 1794 London – 20 Mar 1842 London) cr. Earl 4 Jun 1831
= 18 Oct 1819 London; **Mary Wyndham** (… - 3 Dec 1842 Middlesex) natural daughter of George Wyndham, 3rd Earl of Egremont & Elizabeth Ilive
  A. **Lady Adelaide** Georgiana **FitzClarence** (28 Aug 1820 Bushy Park, Middlesex – 11 Oct 1883 Hove, Sussex)
  B. **Lady Augusta** Margaret **FitzClarence** (29 Jul 1822 Bushy Park – 5 Sep 1846 Gimmersta, Sweden)
  = 10 Apr 1844 Paris; **Baron Knut** Filip **Bonde** (9 Mar 1815 Eriksberg, Sweden – 17 Oct 1871 Stockholm) son of Baron Carl Bonde & Agneta Hildebrand; =2nd Helena Robinson
    1. **Baroness** Adelaide **Augusta Bonde** (30 Aug 1846 Gimmersta – 4 Mar 1872 Stockholm)
    = 2 May 1865 Stockholm; **Count Gustave Fouché, Duke d'Otrante** (17 Jun 1840 Paris – 5 Aug 1910 Stjarnholm) son of Count Athanese Fouché, Duke d'Otrante & Baroness Adelheid von Stedingk; suc.father as Duke 10 Feb 1886; =2nd Baroness Therese von Stedingke
      a. **Augustine Fouché d'Otrante** (2 May 1866 Paris – 12 Nov 1943 Stockholm)
      = 14 Oct 1893 Stockholm; **Frederik** Mauritz **Peyron** (2 Jul 1861 Karlskrona – 8 Jan 1915 Stockholm) son of Edvard Peyron & Katinka Due
        I) **Maud** Therese Anna **Peyron** (15 Mar 1895 Stockholm -

1977)
II) **Victor** Oscar Knut Gustaf **Peyron** (16 Sep 1897 Stockholm – Sep 1971 Stockholm)
= 12 Jul 1922 Stegeborg; **Dagmar Westerberg** (29 Dec 1902 Goteborg – 10 Oct 1990 Stockholm)
  A) **Frederik Peyron** (*8 Sep 1923 Stockholm)
    = 13 Nov 1951 Memphis, Tennessee; **Gertrud Carlsson** (*27 Dec 1922 Paskallavik) daughter of John Carlsson & Tekla Nygren
    1) **Elisabeth Peyron** (*7 Jul 1953 Worcester, Massachusetts)
    2) Fredrik **Edward Peyron** (*10 Jun 1955 Worcester)
      = 22 June 1982; **Susan Ludwig** (*29 Feb 1956)
      a) **Sarah** Elisabeth **Peyron** (*7 Nov 1983 Mancherster, New Hampshire)
        = 30 May 2009; **Hugh** Goodwin **Murphy** (...)
  B) **Christina Peyron** (*24 Dec 1924 Stockholm)
  C) **Carl-Gustaf Peyron** (6 Apr 1928 Stockholm – 4 Sep 1947 Stockholm)
III) **Adine Peyron** (6 Feb 1900 Stockholm – Aug 1989 Stockholm)
= 2 Aug 1931 Stockholm; **Ragnar** Adolf **Wollert** (25 Jul 1886 – Sep 1967 Stockholm) son of Rudolf Wollert & Fanny ...
  A) **Rolf** Ragnar **Wollert** (*26 Nov 1932 Stockholm)
    = 23 Jun 1957 Copenhagen; **Inger Lise Steen** (28 Jul 1932 Copenhagen – 25 Aug 2008 Mellbystrand, Sweden)
    1) **Madeleine** Louise **Wollert** (*3 Mar 1967 Göteborg)
      = 2001; **Imad Abou Daher** (*11 May 1966 Beirut, Lebanon) no issue

C. **William** George **FitzClarence, 2nd Earl of Munster** etc.(19 May 1824 Bushy Park – 30 Apr 1901 Brighton) suc.father as Earl 20 Mar 1842
= 17 Apr 1855 Knightsbridge; (his first cousin) **Wilhelmina Kennedy-Erskine** (27 Jun 1930 – 9 Oct 1906 Brighton) daughter of Hon. John Kennedy-Erskine & Lady Augusta FitzClarence *see below*
1. **Edward, Viscount FitzClarence** (29 Mar 1856 London – 20 Nov 1870 Hove, Sussex)
2. **Hon. Lionel** Frederick Archibald **FitzClarence** (24 Jul 1857 London – 24 Mar 1863 London)
3. **Geoffrey** George Gordon **FitzClarence, 3rd Earl of Munster** etc. (8 Jul 1859 London – 2 Feb 1902 in South Africa) suc.father as Earl

   30 Apr 1901
4. **Hon. Arthur** Falkland Manners **FitzClarence** (18 Oct 1860 Edinburgh – 20 Apr 1861 Edinburgh)
5. **Aubrey FitzClarence, 4**th **Earl of Munster** etc.(7 Jun 1862 London – 1 Jan 1928) suc.brother as Earl 2 Feb 1902
6. **Hon. William** George **FitzClarence** (17 Sep 1864 Hove – 4 Oct 1899)
  = 1887; **Charlotte** Elizabeth Alice **Williams** (1859 – 5 Sep 1902) daughter of Richard Williams
  a. **Dorothy** Margaret Aline **FitzClarence** (23 Sep 1888 East Preston - 1952)
    = 11 Sep 1909 Shoreham; Cecil **Cadogan Elborough** (1885 London - 1953) son of Alfred Elborough & Fanny Hadlands
   I) **Wilhelmina** Susan **Elborough** (7 Aug 1910 Lancing, Sussex - 1970)
   II) William **George** Edward **Elborough** (1912 Lewisham, Kent - Dec 1993)
    = 1937 Rochfort, Essex; **Joan O'Grady** (*1918 Essex) daughter of Hugh O'Grady & Nora Jarvis
   A) George **Patrick** A **Elborough** (*1937)
    = 1961 Brighton; **Rosemary McQuaker** (*12 Oct 1940)
    1) **Nicholas J Elborough** (*10 Jan 1964)
     =1 Nov 1986 (dv.); **Sally Alexander** (...)
     =2 Apr 1997; **Katherine Duchesne** (...)
     issue of 1st:
     a) **Charlotte** Blue **Elborough** (*17 Jun 1986)
     b) **Tobias** George **Elborough** (*Sep 1989)
     c) **Charlie** James **Elborough** (*Aug 1994)
     issue of 2nd:
     d) **Zachary** Roderick **Elborough** (*31 Jul 1997 Winchester, Hampshire)
     e) **Madeleine** Rose **Elborough** (*2000 Winchester)
     f) **Bella Elborough** (*...)
    2) **Philip** Alan **Elborough** (*27 Feb 1966)
     = Oct 1999; **Michelle Treacher** (...)
     a) **Joshua** Alan **Elborough** (*6 May 1988)
    3) **Michael** Patrick **Elborough** (*19 Sep 1968)
     = ...; **Judy Larsson** (...)
     a) **Jasper Elborough** (...)
     b) **Tonto Elborough** (...)
     c) **Brianna Elborough** (...)

B) **Roger** J E **Elborough** (*1940 Essex)
   =1 1961; **Gillian Breaker** (1940 - Jan 1985)
   =2 1986; **Lynda** ... (...)
   issue of 1st:
   1) **Julie Elborough** (*1965)
      = Jul 1993; **Sunil Coutinho** (...)
   2) **Alan Elborough** (*27 Jan 1967)
C) **Anthony** M J **Elborough** (*1941 Sussex)
   = 1968; **Gillian Allen** (..)
   1) **Travis** Darren **Elborough** (*1971)
   2) **Justin** Dale **Elborough** (*13 Sep 1973)
      = Aug 2002; **Helen Norton** (...)
   3) **Saffron** Fay **Elborough** (*1976)
D) **David** William Cadogan **Elborough** (*4 Oct 1942)
   = 1965; **Brenda Sharman** (...)
   1) **Amanda** J **Elborough** (*2 Jun 1965)
      = May 1998 (dv.); **Martin Cannard** (...)
      a) **Jacob** William George **Cannard** (*15 Jan 1999)
E) **Michael** G **Elborough** (*1945)
   =1 1967; **Theresa Woodford** (*1949 London) daughter of Roy Woodford & Helena Light
   =2 1993; **Kay Reynolds** (...)
   issue of 1st:
   1) **Heide** Helena **Elborough** (*1968)
      = Aug 1987; **Craig Barnes** (...)
      a) **Luke** Craig **Barnes** (*Oct 1988)
      b) **Thomas** Michael **Barnes** (*Nov 1989)
      c) **George** Francis **Barnes** (*Mar 2003)
   2) **Jonathan** Michael **Elborough** (*1971)
F) **Jayne Elborough** (*1951 Sussex)
   =1 1970; **Malcolm Wright** (...)
   =2 Dec 1985; **Lloyd Southern** (*1954) son of William Southern & Hazel North
   issue ?
III) **Dorothy** Katherine Elizabeth **Elborough** (1914 Hove - 2005)
   =1 1936 Sussex; **Alan** M **Adamson** (1913 - ...)
   =2 ...; **John O'Grady** (... – 8 Apr 2009 Southwark)
   issue of 1st:
   A) **Alan** H **Adamson** (*1938)
   B) **Janet** A **Adamson** (*1943)

issue of 2nd:
  A) **Linda O'Grady** (...) [married with children]
IV) **Edward** Frederick Fitzclarence **Elborough** (1919 West Derby - Aug 1995)
=1 1945; **Mabel** F **Instrall** (1919 -) daughter of Albert Instrall & Elizabeth Veale
=2 1968; **Ivy** Kathleen **Carter** (1927 - 1973)
issue of 1st (none by 2nd):
  A) **Michael** J **Elborough** (*1948 Sussex)
  B) **John** A **Elborough** (*1953)
    = 1977; **Julie Bridger** (*1957) dau of Frank Bridger & Gladys Nicolaides
    1) **Daniel** Lee **Elborough** (*Mar 1974)
    2) **Mark** Duncan J **Elborough** (*Mar 1978)
  C) **Peter** K **Elborough** (*1956)
    = 1979; **Maureen Budgen** (*1958)
    1) **Natalie Elborough** (*Jun 1983) (twin)
    2) **Sarah Elborough** (*Jun 1983) (twin)
V) **Patrick** Cecil **Elborough** (1920 Hove – 25 Sep 1934 East Grinstead, East Sussex)

b. **Wilhelmina** Violet Eileen **FitzClarence** (17 Jul 1894 – 12 Feb 1962 Thorpe Malsor Hall, Kettering, Northamptonshire)
= 19 Jan 1918 London; **Cecil** John Cokayne **Maunsell** (2 Feb 1881 – 11 Feb 1948 Thorpe Malsor Hall) son of Thomas Maunsell & Catherine Cavendish
  I) **Cecilia** Violet Cokayne **Maunsell** (24 Feb 1919 – 11 Jan 2001 Thorpe Malsor Hall)
    = 12 Oct 1940 Rothwell, Leeds (dv.1958); **George** Arnold Ford **Kennard** (later 3rd Baronet) (27 Apr 1915 – 13 Dec 1999 London) son of Sir Coleridge Kennard, 1st Baronet & Dorothy Barclay; suc.brother as Baronet 3 May 1967; =2nd Mollie Wyllie; =3rd Nicola Carew; =4th Georgina Wernher; upon his death the Baronetage became extinct
    A) **Zandra Kennard** (*17 Jun 1941 Thorpe Malsor Hall)
      = 18 Aug 1962 Rothwell; **John** Middleton Neilson **Powell** (*10 Nov 1936 London) son of John Powell & Fortune Middleton
      1) **Edward** Coleridge Cokayne **Powell** (*2 Feb 1964)
      2) **Louise** Cecilia Middleton **Powell** (*20 Nov 1966 Northampton)
        = 30 Jul 1994 Rothwell; **Crispin** David Jermyn **Holborow**

(*7 Mar 1963 Truro) son of Geoffrey Holborow & Lady Mary Stopford
   a) **George** Maunsell Jermyn **Holborow** (*21 Jun 1997)
   b) **William Holborow** (*18 Apr 1999)
   c) **Benjamin Holborow** (*22 Apr 2003)

7. **Hon. Harold** Edward **FitzClarence** (15 Nov 1870 Hove – 28 Aug 1926)
= 14 May 1902; **Frances** Isabel Eleanor **Keppel** (20 Jul 1874 Mitford, Norfolk – 1 Feb 1951) daughter of William Keppel & Hon. Charlotte Fraser
Issue was raised to the rank of children of an Earl 1928:

a. **Lady** Wilhelmina **Joan** Mary **FitzClarence** (17 Nov 1904 - 1992 Little Massingham, Norfolk)
=1 21 Apr 1928; **Oliver Birkbeck** (6 May 1893 Henstead, Norfolk – 27 May 1952) son of Edward Birkbeck & Emily Seymour
=2 28 Apr 1961; **Henry** John **Cator** (23 Jan 1923 – 27 Mar 1965) son of John Cator & Maud Adeane
issue of 1st (none by 2nd):

I) **Edward** Harold **Birkbeck** (2 May 1929 Little Massingham– 9 Feb 2005 Dumfries)
= 11 Jun 1958; **Sarah** Anne **Brook** (*9 Aug 1934) daughter of Edward Brook & Hon. Catherine Gretton
  A) **Elizabeth** Mary **Birkbeck** (*17 Oct 1960 Bowley Court, Herfordshire)
  B) **Nicola** Susan **Birkbeck** (*2 Dec 1962 Skeffington Hall, Leicestershire)
  C) **George** Charles Edward **Birkbeck** (*8 Dec 1964 Skeffington Hall)
  = 4 Sep 1998 London; **Fiona Gamble** (…)
    1) a son (*19.5.2004)

II) **Mary** Joan **Birkbeck** (*13 Sep 1931 Litle Massingham)

III) **John** Oliver Charles **Birkbeck** (*22 Jun 1936 Little Massingham)
= 2 May 1964; **Hermoine** Anne **Dawes** (*5 Dec 1941 Ainderby, Yorkshire) daughter of D'Arcy Dawes & Naomi Thompson
  A) **Lucy** Claire **Birkbeck** (*7 Oct 1966 Kench Hill, Kent)
  = 8 Jul 1995 Litcham, Norfolk; **Robert Leitao** (*1963)
    1) **Felix** Edward **Leitao** (*Jul 1998 London)
    2) **Tobias** Alexander **Leitao** (*Sep 1999 London)
    3) **Hermione** Sophie **Leitao** (*Jul 2003 London)

            B) **Oliver** Benjamin **Birkbeck** (*3 Apr 1973 Norwich)
            C) **Rosanna** Mary **Birckbeck** (*11 Sep 1974 Norwich)
               = 5 Jul 2003 Litcham; **Michael** W **Tremayne** (*1974 London) son of John Tremayne & Vivienne Cullimore
               1) **Emily** Rose **Tremayne** (*15 Jul 2004 London)
               2) **Benjamin** William **Tremayne** (*31 Mar 2006 London)
         b. **Sir Geoffrey** William Richard Hugh **FitzClarence KBE, 5th Earl of Munster** etc.(17 Feb 1906 – 27 Aug 1975) suc.uncle as Earl 1 Jan 1928; KBE 1957
            = 9 Jul 1928; **Hillary Wilson** (19 Mar 1903 – 29 Oct 1979 Bletchingley, Surrey) daughter of Edward Wilson & Adela Hacket
            no issue
      8. **Lady Lilian** Adelaide Katherine Mary **FitzClarence** (10 Dec 1873 Hove – 15 Jul 1948)
         = 17 Jan 1893 Brighton; **William** Arthur Edward **Boyd** (6 Apr 1845 – 6 Dec 1931) son of Curwen Boyd & Margaret Campbell
         a. **Phyllis** Meata **Boyd** (1894 – 19 Mar 1943)
            = 17 Jan 1922 (dv.); **Viscount Henri** Louis Leon **de Janzé** (…) son of Viscount François Leon de Janzé & …
            no issue
         b. **Benjamin** Harold Alan **Boyd** (16 Dec 1912 – 22 Nov 1930)
      9. **Lady Dorothea** Augusta **FitzClarence** (5 May 1876 Hove – 28 Jan 1942 Hereford)
         = 20 Nov 1899 London; **Chandos** Brydges **Lee-Warner** (11 Jun 1863 – 1 Oct 1944 Hereford)
         a. Dorothy **Jean** Mary Essex **Lee-Warner** (21 Nov 1900 Steyning - …)
         b. Olive **Irene** Wilhelmina **Lee-Warner** (31 May 1902 Steyning– 11 Mar 1975 Herford)
   D. **Hon. Frederick** Charles George **FitzClarence-Hunloke** (1 Feb 1826 – 17 Dec 1878) assumed additional name Hunloke 1865
      = 2 Dec 1856 Penhurst, Kent; (his first cousin) **Hon. Adelaide** Augusta Wilhelmina **Sidney** (1 Jun 1826 Dingerworth, Derbyshire – 20 Sep 1904) daughter of Philip Sidney, 1st Baron De L'Isle & Lady Sophia FitzClarence *see below*
      no issue
   E. **Lady Mary** Gertrude **FitzClarence** (31 Oct - … Nov 1834 London)
   F. **Hon. George FitzClarence** (15 Apr 1836 London – 24 Mar 1894 Uxbridge, Middlesex)
      = 5 Jul 1864 London; **Lady Maria** Henrietta **Scott** (1841 – 27 Jul

1912) daughter of John Scott, 3rd Earl of Clonmell & Hon. Anne de Burgh
1. **Charles FitzClarence** (8 May 1864 Bishopscourt, co. Kildare – 12 Nov 1914 Ypres) killed in action (twin)
= 20 Apr 1898; **Violet Churchill** (11 Jun 1864 London – 22 Dec 1941 Buckingham) daughter of Lord Alfred Churchill & Hon. Harriet Hester

  a. **Edward** Charles **FitzClarence, 6th Earl of Munster** etc.(3 Oct 1899 London – 15 Nov 1983) suc. 2nd cousin as Earl 27 Aug 1975
=1 30 Jul 1925 (dv.1930); **Monica** Sheila Harrington **Grayson** (1907 - 5 Oct 1958) daughter of Sir Henry Grayson, 1st Baronet & Dora Harrington; =2nd Robert Symonds
=2 28 Sep 1939; **Vivian Scholfield** (14 Jul 1908 – 7 May 2008) daughter of Benjamin Scholfield & …
issue of 1st:

  I) **Anthony** Charles **FitzClarence, 7th Earl of Munster** etc.(21 Mar 1926 Dorking, Surrey – 30 Dec 2001 London) suc. father as Earl 15 Nov 1983; upon his death his titles became extinct
=1 28 Jul 1949 London (dv.1966); Louise Marguerite **Diane Delvigne** (*10 May 1923 Liège, Belgium) daughter of Louis Delvigne & Margaret Waite
=2 18 Jun 1966 (dv.1979); **Pamela** Margaret **Spooner** (1921 - 2000) daughter of Arthur Spooner & Evelyn Hinckley; =1st … Hyde
=3 1979; Dorothy **Alexa Maxwell** (22 Dec 1924 – 13 Jun 1995) daughter of Edward Maxwell & Sybil Lubbock
=4 3 May 1997 Cowhurst, Surrey; **Halina Winska**[4] (…) daughter of Mieczlaw Winski-Lubicz
issue of 1st:

  A) **Lady Tara** Francesa **FitzClarence** (*6 Aug 1952 Paris)
= 22 Apr 1979 London; **Ross** Jean **Heffler** (10 Nov 1952 London) son of Leon Heffler & Elizabeth Defries
    1) **Alexandra** Louise **Heffler** (*1 Nov 1982 London)
    2) **Leo** Edward Michael **Heffler** (*17 Dec 1985 London)
  B) **Lady Finola** Dominique **FitzClarence** (*6 Dec 1953)
= 1981 (dv.2007); **Jonathan** Terence **Poynton** (*1957) son of Desmond Poynton & Nancy Eva
    1) **Chloe** Nona **Poynton** (*29 May 1982)

---

[4] Halina, Countess of Munster had a daughter by a previous relationship who took the FitzClarence name but was not a child, and not adopted, by the 7th Earl.

      2) **Oliver** Maximilian Christo **Poynton** (*20 Jun 1984)
    issue of 2nd:
   C) **Charlotte** Catherine **Lawrence Mills** (*1964) née Oonaugh Sarah FitzClarence; adopted 1965 by John Lawrence Mills
    = … 1987; **Raymond Burt** (…)
    1) **Christopher** James **Burt** (*1987)
    2) **Jennifer** Emily **Burt** (*1989)
    3) **Stephanie** Louise **Burt** (*1991)
   D) **Lady Georgina FitzClarence** (*19 Dec 1966)
    =1 1993 (dv.1995); **Paul** Robert **Phillips** (…) son of Peter Phillips
    =2 1997; **John Adam** (…)
    issue of 2nd (none by 1st):
    1) **Thomas** Charles **Adam** (*31 Mar 1999)
  II) **Lady Mary-Jill FitzClarence** (6 Feb 1928 – 17 Jan 1971)
    =1 4 Jun 1953 (ann.1960); **Melvin Flyer** (…)
    =2 28 Mar 1968; **John Walter** (31 Oct 1908 - 1980) son of John Walter & Charlotte Foster; =1st Florence Cole
    no issue
 b. **Joan** Harriet **FitzClarence** (23 Dec 1901 – 6 Jan 1971)
  = 30 Mar 1933 London; **Francis Barchard** (1903 Sussex - 25 Nov 1941) killed in action; son of Francis Barchard & Emma Lawrence
   I) **Jane** Ann Violet **Barchard** (*5 Nov 1935)
    =1 10 Mar 1962; **Geoffrey** Ewart **Martin** (… - 8 Apr 1978) son of Melton Martin
    =2 9 May 1981; **Alastair** Jackson Wallace **Reid** (...)
    A) **Lucinda** Katharine **Martin** (*20 Oct 1966)
      = 17 Feb 1990; **Peter Williams** (…)
      1) **Sophie** Elizabeth Rose **Williams** (*30 May 1992)
      2) **Eleanor** Jane **Williams** (*3 Mar 2000)
   II) **Elizabeth** Maud **Barchard** (*18 Apr 1939)
    = 13 Jul 1967; **David** Leslie **Scott** (…) son of Thomas Scott
    A) **Juliet** Catherine **Scott** (*23 Nov 1968)
    B) **Sara** Frances **Scott** (*16 Dec 1970)
2. **Edward FitzClarence** (8 May 1864 Bishopscourt, co. Kildare – 7 Aug 1897 Abu-Hamed, Sudan) (twin) killed in action
3. **William** Henry **FitzClarence** (17 Dec 1868 – 24 Nov 1921)
  = 11 Aug 1908 London; **Hilda** Charlotte **Sankey** (1876 Thanet, Kent - 3 Jan 1959) daughter of Richard Sankey
  no issue

4. **Lionel** Ashley Arthur **FitzClarence** (30 Nov 1870 London – 19 Dec 1936 the Crimea)
= 16 Jul 1913; **Theodora** Frances Maclean **Jack** (1880 London – 12 Apr 1948) daughter of Evan Jack
   a. **Mary** Theodora Annette **FitzClarence** (10 May 1914 – 14 Aug 2002 Chichester, Sussex)
   = 1948; **Adam Gluskiewicz** (…)
   I) **Anna** Judith **Gluszkiewicz** (*28 Oct 1949)
5. **Annette** Mary **FitzClarence** (15 Jun 1873 London – 7 Jul 1970)
6. **Mary FitzClarence** (17 Aug 1877 London – 19 Feb 1939 Lyndhurst, Hampshire)
= 5 Oct 1905 London; **Frederick** Drummund Vincent **Wing** (29 Nov 1860 Christchurch, Hampshire – 2 Oct 1915 in France) killed in action; son of Vincent Wing & Gertrude Vane
   a. **Gertrude** Iris **Wing** (1 Aug 1906 London - 28 Jul 1983 Milford-on-Sea, Hampshire)

G. **Hon. Edward FitzClarence** (8 Jul 1837 London – 23 Jul 1855 Redan, Crimea) died of wounds received in battle

II. **Lady Sophia FitzClarence** (4 Mar 1795 London – 10 Apr 1837 Kensington Palace, London)
= 13 Aug 1825 London; **Sir Philip** Charles **Sidney, 2nd Baronet, 1st Baron De L'Isle and Dudley, GCH** (11 Mar 1800 Penhurst, Kent – 4 Mar 1851 Penhurst) son of Sir John Shelley-Sidney, 1st Baronet & Henrietta Hunloke; cr. Baron 13 Jan 1835, suc.father as Baronet 14 Mar 1849; GCH 1831

A. **Hon. Adelaide** Augusta Wilhelmina **Sidney** (1 Jun 1826 Dingerworth, Derbyshire – 20 Sep 1904)
= 2 Feb 1856 Penhurst Place; (her first cousin) **Hon. Frederick** Charles George **FitzClarence-Hunloke** (1 Feb 1826 – 17 Dec 1878) son of George FitzClarence, 1st Earl of Munster & Mary Wyndham *see above*
no issue

B. **Sir Philip Sidney, 2nd Baron De L'Isle and Dudley, 3rd Baronet** (29 Jan 1828 London – 17 Feb 1898 London) suc.father as Baron and Baronet 4 Mar 1851
=1 23 Apr 1850 London; **Mary Foulis** (19 May 1826 Ingleby, Yorkshire – 14.6.1891 London) daughter of Sir William Foulis, 8th Baronet & Mary Ross
=2 25 Jan 1893 London; Emily **Frances Ramsay** (1864 Brackely, Northamptonshire – 3 Nov 1926) daughter of William Ramsay & Emily Tredcroft; =2nd Sir Walter Stirling, 3rd Baronet

issue of 1ˢᵗ (none by 2ⁿᵈ):
1. **Hon. Mary** Sophia **Sidney** (5 May 1851 London – 25 Nov 1903 London)
2. **Sir Philip Sidney, 3ʳᵈ Baron De L'Isle and Dudley, 4ᵗʰ Baronet** (14 May 1853 London – 24 Dec 1922) suc. father as Baron etc. 17 Feb 1898
   = 12 Jun 1902 London; **Hon. Elizabeth** Maria **Vereker** (26 Nov 1860 London – 19 Jul 1958) daughter of Standish Vereker, 4ᵗʰ Viscount Gort & Hon. Caroline Gage; =1ˢᵗ William Astell
   no issue
3. **Sir Algernon Sidney, 4ᵗʰ Baron De L'Isle and Dudley, 5ᵗʰ Baronet** (11 Jun 1854 Penhurst – 18 Apr 1945) suc.brother as Baron etc. 24 Dec 1922
4. **Hon. Henry Sidney** (17 Jan 1858 London – 13 Apr 1896 Durham)
5. **Sir William Sidney, 5ᵗʰ Baron De L'Isle and Dudley, 6ᵗʰ Baronet** (19 Aug 1859 London – 18 Jun 1945) suc.brother as Baron etc.18 Apr 1945
   = 5 Dec 1905 London; **Winifred** Augusta **Yorke Bevan** (1874 – 11 Feb 1959) daughter of Roland Yorke Bevan & Hon. Agneta Kinnaird
   a. **Hon. Mary** Olivia **Sidney** (20 Nov 1906 London – 24 Nov 1959)
      = 3 Jun 1939; **Walter** Hugh Stewart **Garnett** (1875 -)
      son of Frank Garnett & Jeanne Buddicom; =1ˢᵗ Enid Evans
      I) **Andrew** William **Garnett** (*31 Aug 1943)
         = 24 Aug 1968 London; **Maria Constantinidou** (*1946) daughter of Noikis Constantinides
         A) **Tara** Olivia **Garnett** (*1969 London)
            = May 2002 London; **Benjamin** J **Glasstone** (*1970)
            1) **Ezra** Daniel **Glasstone** (*May 1998 London)
            2) **Rachel** Deborah **Glasstone** (*Nov 2001 London)
         B) **Michael** Nicholas **Garnett** (*1981 London)
   b. **Sir William** Philip **Sidney KG, GCMG, GCVO, 1ˢᵗ Viscount De L'Isle, 6ᵗʰ Baron De L'Isle and Dudley, 7ᵗʰ and 9ᵗʰ Baronet** (23 May 1909 London – 5 Apr 1991 London) suc. father as Baron etc.18 Jun 1945; cr. Viscount 12 Jan 1956 suc. distant cousin, Sir Sidney Shelley as 9ᵗʰ Baronet 25 Jul 1965; Governor-General of Astralia 1961-1965
      =1 8 Jun 1940 London; **Hon. Jacqueline** Corinne Yvonne

Vereker[5] (20 Oct 1914 London – 15 Nov 1962 London) daughter of John Vereker, 6th Viscount Gort & Corinne Vereker[6]
=2 24 Mar 1966 Paris; **Margaret** Eldrydd **Shoubridge** (1913 Chester – 22 Jan 2002 Crickhowell, Wales) daughter of Thomas Shoubridge & … Dugdale; =1st Wilfred Bailey, 3rd Baron Glanusk
issue of 1st:

I) **Hon. Elizabeth** Sophia **Sidney** (*12 Mar 1941)
=1 10 Oct 1959 (dv.1966); George Silver **Oliver** Annesley **Colthurst** (1 Mar 1931 - 16 Aug 2008 Beaulieu, France) son of Sir Richard Colhurst, 8th Baronet & Denys West; =2nd Caroline Combe
=2 1 Jul 1966 (dv.1971); **Sir** Edward **Humphrey** Tyrell **Wakefield, 2nd Baronet** (*11 Jul 1936) son of Sir Edward Wakefield, 1st Baronet & Lalage Thompson; =1st Priscilla Bagot and =3rd Hon. Katharine Baring
=3 26 Jan 1972 Gibralter (dv.1989); **James** Sylvester **Rattray of Rattray** (3 Aug 1919 – 1999) son of Paul Burman-Clerk-Rattray
=4 Nov 1989 London; Robert **Samuel** Clive **Abel Smith** (*17 Apr 1936)
issue of 1st:

  A) **Shaunagh** Anne Henrietta **Colthurst** (*30 Apr 1961)
=1 1980 Shropshire (dv.1990); **Thomas** Peter William **Heneage** (*1950) son of Peter Heneage & Jean Douglas; =2nd Carol Vogel
=2 2 Aug 1995; **Crispin** James Alan Nevill **Money-Coutts, 9th Baron Latymer** (*8 Mar 1955) son of Hugo Money-Coutts, 8th Baron Latymer & Hon. Penelope Emmet; =1st Hon. Lucy Deedes; suc.father as Baron 10 Nov 2003
issue of 1st (none by 2nd):

    1) **Elizabeth** Anne Sophia **Heneage** (*1981)
= 2006; **Hon. Quintin** John Neil Martin **Hogg** (*1973) son of Rt.Hon. Douglas Hogg, 3rd Viscount Hailsham & Sarah Boyd-Carpenter, (life) Baroness Hogg; heir apparent to father

      a) **Eleanor Hogg** (*Nov 2010)

    2) **Henry** Robert **Heneage** (*1983)
issue of 2nd:

  B) **Maximilian** Edward Vereker **Wakefield** (*22 Feb 1967

---

[5] Jacqueline was the grand-niece of Elizabeth, Baroness De L'Isle.
[6] The 6th Viscount Gort and his wife were first cousins to one another.

Lough Coltra Castle, Gort) heir-apparent to Baronetcy
= 5 Nov 1994 Winchester; **Lucinda** Catherine **Pipe**
(*1969) daughter of David Pipe & Patricia Coombes
  1) **William Wakefield** (*9 May 1998)
  2) **Edward** Gort **Wakefield** (*22 Jun 2000)
 issue of 3rd (none by 4th):
C) **Robert** Surtees Predergast **Rattray** (*11 Oct 1972)
D) a daughter (*25 Mar 1983)
II) **Hon. Catherine** Mary **Sidney** (*20 Oct 1942)
=1 1 Dec 1964¹ Canberra, Australia (dv.1983); Martin **John Wilbraham** (*3 Jun 1931 London) son of Edward Wilbraham & Evelyn Martin
=2 9 May 1983; **Nicholas** Hyde **Villiers** (10 Apr 1939 – 31 Aug 1998 at sea) son of Sir Charles Villiers & Pamela Flower
=3 Nov 2002 London; **Nigel** Samuel **Wass** (*1942) son of Lawrence Wass & Margaret Wilson; =1st Sean Oyler
issue of 1st (none by others):
A) **Alexander** John **Wilbraham** (*22 Oct 1965 Cheshire)
  = 3 Sep 1996; **Fernanda Amaral Valentini** (…) daughter of Arnoldo Valentini & Valeria Amaral
  1) **Marina Wilbraham** (*31 Jan 1997) (twin)
  2) **Camilla Wilbraham** (*31 Jan 1997) (twin)
B) **Rupert** Edward Robert **Wilbraham** (*26 Feb 1967 Cheshire)
  = 14 Jun 2007 Moscow; **Anna Yevdokimova** (*4 Jun 1973) daughter of Oleg Yevdokimov & Ludilla …
  no issue
C) **Jocelyn** Thomas Ralph **Wilbraham** (*30 Apr 1970 Cheshire)
  = 24 Jun 2005 London; **Fiona Butler-Adams** (*9 Jul 1973) daughter of David Butler-Adams & Rosalie Bradshaw
  1) **Oscar** David John **Wilbraham** (*25 Jul 2006)
III) **Sir Philip** John Algernon **Sidney, 2nd Viscount De L'Isle, 7th Baron De L'Isle and Dudley, 8th & 10th Baronet** (*21 Apr 1945 Dailly, Scotland) suc.father as Viscount etc.5 Apr 1991
= 15 Nov 1980 Penhurst; **Isobel** Tresyllian **Compton** (*18 Mar 1950 London) daughter of Sir Edmund Compton & Betty Williams

131

    A) **Hon. Sophia** Jacqueline Mary **Sidney** (*25 Mar 1983 London)
    B) **Hon. Philip** William Edmund **Sidney** (*2 Apr 1985 London) heir apparent to father
IV) **Hon. Anne** Marjorie **Sidney** (*15 Aug 1947 Penhurst, Kent)
= 3 Jun 1967 Penhurst; **David** Alexander **Harries** (*14 Apr 1938 Sydney, Australia) son of David Harries & Margaret Street
    A) **Alexandra** Victoria Corinna **Harries** (*12 Jul 1968 Long Beach, California[7])
= 19 Jun 2004 Benenden; **Piers** Adrian Carlyle **Hillier** (*24 Sep 1968 Nassau, Bahamas) son of Philip Hillier & Geraldine Matthews
    1) **Hugh** Alexander Philip **Hillier** (*29 Jun 2005 London)
    2) **Penelope** Elizabeth Anne **Hillier** (*23 Jan 2008 London)
    3) **Audrey** Camilla Hester **Hillier** (*24 Sep 2009 London)
    B) David **Henry Harries** (*4 May 1970 Sydney, Australia)
= 14 Dec 2001 London; **Sophy** Emma **Maclean** (*15 Feb 1972) daughter of Roddy Maclean & Hon. Sarah Corbett
    1) **Lara** Constance **Harries** (*25 Mar 2004 London)
    2) **Miranda** Violet **Harries** (*17 May 2006 London)
    3) **David** Edward **Harries** (*7 Apr 2010 London)
    C) **James** Hugh **Harries** (*28 Jun 1972 London[8])
= 19 Sep 2003 London; **Harriet** Florence **Pugh** (*6 Mar 1973) daughter of Richard Pugh & Diana Coley
    1) **Robert** Alexander **Harries** (*18 Jun 2008 London) (twin)
    2) **Charles** Richard **Harries** (*18 Jun 2008 London) (twin)
V) **Hon. Lucy** Corinna Agneta **Sidney** (*21 Feb 1953 Tonbridge)
= 26 Feb 1974 Tonbridge; **Hon. Michael** Charles James **Willoughby** (*14 Jul 1948 London) son of Michael Willoughby, 12th Baron Middleton & Janet Cornwall; heir-

---

[7] Most sources say Alexandra was born in San Diego, but her father clarified it was Long Beach.
[8] Again, James' father corrected published sources which state James was born in Ashford, Kent.

apparent to Barony
  A) **James** William Michael **Willoughby** (*8 Mar 1976 York)
= 10 Sep 2005 Petworth, Sussex; **Lady Cara** Mary Cecilia **Boyle** (*16 Jun 1976 Winchester, Hampshire) daughter of John Boyle, 15th Earl of Cork and Orrery & Hon. Rebecca Noble
    1) **Thomas** Michael Jonathan **Willoughby** (*23 Aug 2007)
    2) **Flora** Rebecca Lucy **Willoughby** (*7 Jan 2009)
    3) due Feb. 2011
  B) **Charlotte** Jacqueline Louise **Willoughby** (*20 Sep 1978 Malton)
= 8 Jul 2006 London; **Martin Taylor** (*21 Jul 1971 East Kilbride, Lanarkshire) son of James Taylor
    1) **Matilda** Jacqueline Azvina **Taylor** (*30 Jan 2009)
  C) **Emma** Caralie Sarah **Willoughby** (*7 Sep 1981 Malton)
  D) **Rose** Arabella Julia **Willoughby** (*25 Sep 1984 Malton)
  E) **Charles** Edward Henry **Willoughby** (*27 Jul 1986 Scarborough)

C. **Hon. Ernestine** Wellington **Sidney** (9 Jan 1834 London – 20 Sep 1910 London)
= 9 Jan 1868 London; **Philip Perceval** (19 Mar 1814 London – 28 Mar 1897) son of Alexander Perceval & Jane L'Estrange
 1. **Sir Philip Hunloke, GCVO** (26 Nov 1868 London – 1 Apr 1947 London) (twin) ne Perceval, assumed name Hunloke 1904
= 12 Feb 1892 London; **Silvia Heseltine** (1872 London - 1951 London) daughter of John Heseltine & Sarah Edmundson
  a. **Joan** Cecil **Hunloke** (14 Apr 1901 London - Jan 1991) née Perceval
= 28 Apr 1924 London; **Philip Fleming** (15 Aug 1889 – 13 Oct 1971) son of Robert Fleming
  I) **Anne** Kathleen **Fleming** (4 Jan 1926 - Jul 1996)
= 9 Feb 1952; **Jesse Hughes** (…)
  II) **Silvia** Catriona **Fleming** (14 Feb 1930 - Jun 1987)
= 25 Nov 1951; George **Christopher Rittson-Thomas** (1927 Cardiff - ...) son of Geoffrey Rittson-Thomas & Grace Cotter
    A) **Michael** P **Rittson-Thomas** (*1953 London)
    B) **Hugo Rittson-Thomas** (*1957 London)
= 2009/2010; **Silke Taprogge** (...) daughter of Ludwig Taprogge
    C) **Rupert Rittson-Thomas** (*1963 Oxford)
= ...; **Kate ...** (...)
      1) **Walter** Robert **Rittson-Thomas** (...)

2) **Theodore** George **Rittson-Thomas** (*29 Jun 2009)
III) **Robert Fleming** (*18 Sep 1932)
   = 28 Apr 1962; **Victoria** Margaret **Ackroyd** (*1 Apr 1939)
   A) **Joanna** Kate **Fleming** (*1963)
      = 1997; **James King** (…)
      1) **Elva** Silvie **King** (*1998)
      2) **Valentine** Jack Naisbett **King** (*2000)
   B) **Philip Fleming** (*1965)
      = 1997; **Jane Carter** (…)
      1) **Robert Fleming** (*1998)
      2) **Lorna** Hebe Louise **Fleming** (*2000)
   C) **Rory** David **Fleming** (*1968)
      = 31 Oct 2001 Valdemars Slot, Denmark (dv.2010);
      Baroness Caroline Iuel-Brockdorff (*9 Sep 1975)
      daughter of Baron Niels Iuel-Brockdorff & Margarethe Lundgren
      1) **Alexander** William **Fleming** (*7 Apr 2004 London)
      2) **Josephine** Margarethe Victoria **Fleming** (*20 Dec 2006)
b. **Alberta** Diana **Hunloke** (1898 - 10 Feb 1972) nee Perceval
   = 5 Feb 1921 London; **Sir George** Camborne Beauclerk **Paynter, KCVO** (2 Aug 1880 London – 15 Aug 1950 near Grantham) son of George Paynter & Frances Beauclerk; KCVO 1950
I) **Janetta** Alba **Paynter** (*26 Jan 1922)
   =1 2 Aug 1946 (dv.1948); **Richard** Boycott **Magor** (1918 - Oct 2003) son of Richard Magor & Frances Boycott
   =2 5 May 1954; **John** Anthony **Warre** (4 Dec 1912 London - Sep 1999) son of John Warre & Marie Scott; =1st Arabella Mackintosh
   issue of 1st (none by 2nd):
   A) **Carolyn Magor** (*ca.1947)
      =1 6 Jan 1977 London (dv.); **Broderick** Giles Edward **Munro-Wilson** (…) son of Donald Munro-Wilson; =2nd Samantha Bleby
      =2 Jul 1996; **Michael Peacock** (…)
      issue of 1st:
      1) **Charlotte** Alba Louise **Munro-Wilson** (*26 Nov 1977)
         = 2006; **Ross** Lindsay **Henderson** (…) son of Lindsay Henderson
         a) **Edward** Ross Beauclerk **Henderson** (*9 June 2008)
II) **Yvery** Silvia **Paynter** (*16 Dec 1924)

= 18 Dec 1952 London; **Hamish** Edward Lachlan **Wallace** (*19 Sep 1924) son of Harold Wallace & Elizabeth MacPherson
   A) **James** George Chisholm **Wallace** (*1954)
   B) Elizabeth **Anna** Francesca **Wallace** (*1955)
      =1 2 Dec 1980 (dv.1986); **Hon. John Fermor-Hesketh** (*15 Mar 1953) son of Frederick Fermor-Hesketh, 2nd Baron Hesketh & Christian McEwen; =2nd Helena Hunt
      =2 1991; **Thomas Oates** (…)
      issue of 2nd (none by 1st):
      1) **Ophelia** Rose **Oates** (*1992 London)
   III) **George Paynter** (2 Aug 1933 – 14 Apr 1954 Fayid, Egypt)
c. **Henry** Philip **Hunloke** (27 Dec 1906 London – 13 Jan 1978 London)
   =1 28 Nov 1929 (dv.1945); **Lady Anne Cavendish** (20 Aug 1909 – 1981) daughter of Victor Cavendish, 9th Duke of Devonshire & Lady Evelyn Fitzmaurice; =2nd Christopher Holland-Martin; =3rd Alexander Victor Montagu, 10th Earl of Sandwich[9]
   =2 19 May 1945 (dv.1972); **Virginia** Archer **Clive** (14 Mar 1913 Ludlow – 14 Feb 1995) dau of Percy Clive & Alice Dallas
   =3 1972; **Ruth** Mary **Holdsworth** (1917 - Jun 1998 Marlborough) daughter of Frederick Holdsworth & Mary Arundell; =1st Clarence Percival
   issue of 1st:
   I) **Philippa** Victoria **Hunloke** (10 Dec 1930 London - 20 Jul 2005)
      = 26 Apr 1955 London (dv.1960); **William** Waldorf **Astor, 3rd Viscount Astor** (13 Aug 1907 Cliveden, Buckinghamshire – 8 Mar 1966 Nassau, Bahamas) son of Waldorf Astor, 2nd Viscount Astor & Nancy Langhorne; suc. father as Viscount 30 Sep 1952; he =1st Hon. Sarah Norton, =3rd Bronwen Pugh
      A) **Hon. Emily** Mary **Astor** (*9 Jun 1956)
         =1 1984 (dv.); **Alan Gregory** (…) son of David Gregory
         =2 1988 (dv.1996); **James** Ian **Anderson** (*1 Nov 1952) son of John Anderson & Lady Gillian Drummond
         issue of 2nd (none by 1st):
         1) **Thomas** Alexander **Anderson** (*1990)
         2) **Rory** John **Anderson** (*2 Nov 1991)

---

[9] By her 3rd marriage, Lady Anne became the step-mother of her daughter-in-law, Lady Katherine (Montagu) Hunloke.

      3) **Liza** Kate **Anderson** (*1993) (twin)
      4) **Isobel** Nancy **Anderson** (*1993) (twin)
  II) **Timothy** Henry **Hunloke** (*30 Dec 1932 London)
  III) **Nicholas** Victor **Hunloke** (*22 Apr 1939 London)
    = 15 Jul 1965 London; **Lady Katherine** Victoria **Montagu**
    (*22 Feb 1945 London) daughter of Victor Montagu, 10th Earl of
    Sandwich & Rosemary Peto
    A) **Henrietta** Yvery **Hunloke** (*14 May 1968)
      = 17 Oct 1998; **Lucien** Henry Valentine **Thynne** (*2 June
      1965) son of Lord Valentine Thynne & Veronica Jacks
      1) **Atalanta** Xenia **Thynne** (*27 Dec 2000 London)
      2) **Cassia** Victoria **Thynne** (*15 Jul 2002 London)
    B) **Edward** Perceval **Hunloke** (*1 Nov 1969)
      = 16 Jul 2005 London; **Philippa Collett** (*17 Feb 1965
      Swindon) daughter of David Collett & Glenda Pratt
      1) **Molly** Evelyn **Hunloke** (*6 Feb 1999 London)
      2) **Delilah** Rose **Hunloke** (*4 Dec 2003 London)
    C) **Matilda Hunloke** (*25 Jul 1972 London)
      = 19 Jul 2003; **Edward** William P. **Cartlidge** (*11 Sep 1970
      London) son of William Cartlidge & Denise Rayner
      1) **Wilfred** Victor P. **Cartlidge** (*30 Sep 2004 London)
      2) **Samson** Edward P. **Cartlidge** (*25 Apr 2006 Salisbury)
      3) **Cecily** May **Cartlidge** (*10 Feb 2010 London)
issue of 2nd (none by 3rd):
  IV) **Clare Hunloke** (10 Jan 1947 – 23 Nov 1964)
  V) **Sarah Hunloke** (*17 Apr 1949)
    = …; **Antônio Correa de Sá** (*1950) son of José Correa de Sá
    & Lilias van Waterschoot Pinto da Rocha
    A) **Marta Correa de Sá** (…)
    B) **Inèz Correa de Sá** (…)
    C) **Sofia Correa de Sá** (…)
2. **Kathleen** Sophy **Perceval** (26 Nov 1868 London – 10 Aug 1931
  Yvery, Cowes, Isle of Wight) (twin)
3. **Ernestine Perceval** (6 May 1870 London - 1887 Isle of Wight)
4. **Ernest Perceval** (19 Nov 1871 Hamble, Southampton - ca.1890 in
  Australia)
D. **Hon. Sophia** Philippa **Sidney** (11 Mar 1837 – 12 May 1907)
= 20 Apr 1871 London; **Count Alexander** Friedrich Carl **von Kielmansegg** (13 Aug 1833 Hanover - Aug 1914) son of Count Eduard von Kielmansegg & Juliane von Zesterfleth
no issue

III. **Henry** Edward **FitzClarence** (27 Mar 1796 Bushy Park - Sep 1817 in India)
IV. **Lady Mary FitzClarence** (19 Dec 1798 Bushy Park – 13 Jul 1864 London)
= 19 Jun 1824 London; **Hon. Charles** Richard **Fox** (6 Nov 1796[10] London – 13 Apr 1873 London) son of Henry Fox, 3rd Baron Holland & Elizabeth Vassall
no issue
V. **Lord Sir Frederick FitzClarence, GCH** (9 Dec 1799 Bushy Park – 30 Oct 1854 Glendale, Northumberland)
= 9 May 1821; **Lady Augusta Boyle** (14 Aug 1801 London – 28 Jul 1876 Etal, Northamptonshire) son of George Boyle, 4th Earl of Glasgow & Lady Augusta Hay
 A. **Augusta** Georgiana Frederica **FitzClarence** (Dec 1823/4 Belfast – 18 Oct 1865)
 B. **William** Henry Adolphus **FitzClarence** (16 – 27 Jul 1827 Belfast)
VI. **Lady Elizabeth FitzClarence** (17 Jan 1801 Bushy Park – 16 Jan 1856 Edinburgh)
= 4 Dec 1820 London; **William** George **Hay KT, GCH, 18th Earl of Erroll**, Lord Hay, Lord Stains, **1st Baron Kilmarnock** (21 Feb 1801 Slains Castle, Aberdeenshire – 19 Apr 1846 London) son of William Hay, 17th Earl of Eroll & Alcia Eliot; suc.father as Earl 26 Jan 1819; cr. Baron Kilmarnock 17 Jun 1831; GCH 1830, KT 1834
 A. **Lady** Adelaide **Ida** Harriet Augusta **Hay** (18 Oct 1821 – 22 Oct 1867 Exton, Rutland)
 = 1 Nov 1841 London; **Charles** George **Noel, 2nd Earl of Gainsborough**, Viscount Campden, Baron Noel (5 Sep 1818 – 13 Aug 1881 London) son of Charles Noel, 1st Earl of Gainsborough & Elizabeth Grey; suc. father as Earl 10 Jun 1866
  1. **Lady Blanche** Elizabeth Mary Annunciata **Noel** (22 Mar 1845 - 21 Mar 1881 North Conway, New Hampshire)
  = 6 Mar 1870 London; **Thomas Murphy** (1846 – 11 Oct 1890)
  no issue
  2. **Lady Constance** Julia Eleanor Georgiana **Noel** (19 Oct 1847 London – 8 Apr 1891)
  = 13 Jan 1874 Canterbury; **Sir Alan Henry Bellingham, 4th Baronet** (23 Aug 1846 Bellingham Castle, Louth, Ireland – 9 Jun 1921) son of Sir Alan Bellingham, 3rd Baronet & Elizabeth

---

[10] Charles Fox was born illegitimate but his parents subsequent marriage allowed him ot be styled as a son of a Baron.

Clarke; suc. father as Baronet 19 Apr 1889; =2nd Hon. Leigar de Clifton
a. **Mother** Ida **Mary (Emanuel)** Elizabeth Agnes **Bellingham** (26 Jan 1876 London – 28 Nov 1945 St. Leonards)
b. **Sir Edward** Henry Charles Patrick **Bellingham, 5th Baronet** (26 Jan 1879 Oakham – 19 May 1956 Dublin) suc.father as Baronet 9 Jun 1921
= 11 Jun 1904; **Charlotte** Elizabeth **Payne** (1880 – 25 May 1964 Coptford, Essex) daughter of Alfred Payne & …; =1st Frederick Gough
   I) **Gertrude** Mary **Bellingham** (23 Jul 1906 in Guatemala – 16 May 1983 London)
   = 15 Feb 1927; **Ronald** Derwent **Hawker**[11] (28 Jul 1901 London – 26 Jan 1972) son of Rev. Bertram Hawker & Constance Buxton
     A) **Martin Hawker** (*10 Feb 1929)
c. **Dame Augusta** Mary Monica **Bellingham, DBE** (19 Aug 1880 Oakham – 16 May 1947) DBE 1918
= 6 Jul 1905 Mount Stuart, Isle of Bute; **Sir John Crichton-Stuart KT, 4th Marquess of Bute,** Earl of Windsor, Viscount Montjoy, Baron Cardiff, **9th Earl of Dumfries,** Viscount Ayr, **7th Earl of Bute**, Viscount Kingarth, Lord Mountstuart, Cumra and Inchmarnock, **5th Baron Mount Stuart of Wortley, 17th Lord Crichton** (20 Jun 1881 London – 25 Apr 1947) son of John, 3rd Marquess of Bute & Hon. Gwendolen Fitzalan-Howard; suc. father as Marquess etc. 9 Oct 1890; KT 1922
   I) **Lady Mary Crichton-Stuart** (8 May 1906 Edinburgh - 1980) after her marriage she was known as Lady Mary Stuart-Walker
   = 8 May 1933 London; **Edward** Alan **Walker** (6 Dec 1894 Cambridge - …) son of Arthur Walker & Ellen Church
     A) **Ione** Mary Stuart **Walker** (*3 Aug 1934 Athens, Greece)
     = 23 Jul 1955 London; **Baron Christian** Johan Manuel Marie **von Oppenheim** (4 Feb 1926 Antibes, France – 8 Oct 1967 near Lagos, Nigeria) killed in a car crash; son of Baron Harold von Oppenheim & Manuela de Rivera
       1) **Baroness Corinna** Maria de Roccio Pimpinella Fernanda **von Oppenheim** (*30 May 1956 Madrid)
       = 29 Dec 1983 San Roque, Spain; **William Hettinger** (*30

---

[11] Ronald Hawker is also descended from Dora Bland (aka Mrs. Jordan) via her daughter Lucy (Ford) Hawker (not a child of William IV).

May 1956 Madrid) son of John Hettinger & Elisabeth ...
  a) **Caroline Hettinger** (*5 Dec 1984 New York City)
  b) **Charles Hettinger** (*1 Nov 1986 Pawling, New York)
2) **Baron Eduard** Harold Manuel Maria Rodrigo **von Oppenheim** (*13 Mar 1958 Madrid)
  =1 Aug 1974 Sabeti Spiritu, Argentina (dv.); **Telma Carlini** (...)
  =2 9 May 1980 Madrid; **Ana Maria Fernandez y Smith** (...) daughter of Manuel Fernandez & Shirley Smith
  issue of 1st:
  a) **Baroness Christia von Oppenheim** (*23 May 1975 Sancti Spiritu)
  issue of 2nd:
  b) **Baroness Maria Manuela von Oppenheim** (*31 Aug 1985 Madrid)
  c) **Baroness Maria Almudena von Oppenheim** (*8 Oct 1988 Madrid)
3) **Baroness Flora** Claudia Maria del Mar Monica **von Oppenheim** (*4 May 1960 Madrid)
  = 1991; **Jesus Medrano y Yllera** (...)
  issue ?
4) **Baroness Maria Gabriela** Isabel **von Oppenheim** (*22 Feb 1963 Madrid)
  = 3 Jun 1988 San Roque; **Fidel de Sandagorta y Gomez del Campillo** (...) son of Jesus de Sandagorta & Maria Soledad Gomez del Campillo
  issue ?
B) **Hella** Immaculate Stuart **Walker** (*8 Dec 1935 Athens)
= 3 Jun 1957; **Frederick** Villeneuve **Nicolle** (...) son of Arthur Nicolle
 1) **Miranda** Camilla **Nicolle** (*29 Oct 1958)
   = Aug 1986 London; **Paul Berrow** (...)
   a) **Grace Berrow** (*May 1987 London)
   b) **Augustus** Peter **Berrow** (*Oct 1989 London)
   c) **Daisy** Stuart **Berrow** (*Aug 1992 London)
   d) **Joya Berrow** (*Mar 1994 London)
 2) **Edwina** Mary **Nicolle** (*2 Feb 1961)
   =1 May 1991; **Timothy** M C **Copping** (*1962) son of Austin Copping & Haidee Cockroft
   =2 May 2000 London; **Hon. Alexander** David **Smith**

(*11 Mar 1959) son of William Smith, 4th Viscount Hambleden & Donna Maria Carmela Attolico di Adelfa
issue of 1st (none by 2nd):
  a) **Olivia** Rose A **Copping** (*Jan 1994 York)
  b) **Benedict** Oscar F **Copping** (*Jun 1995 York)
3) **Hugo** Arthur Villeneuve **Nicolle** (*12 Jan 1963)
= Jul 1996; **Rebecca** M **Crawley** (*1965 London) daughter of Eustace Crawley & Dorothy Bacon
  a) **Mamie** Elspeth **Nicolle** (*Oct 1997 London)
  b) **Dora** Rose **Nicolle** (*Aug 1999 London)
  c) **Arthur** Eustace Villaneuve **Nicolle** (*Jul 2003 London)

II) **Sir John Crichton-Stuart KT, 5th Marquess of Bute** etc. (4 Aug 1907 – 14 Aug 1956) suc. father as Marquess 25 Apr 1947
= 26 Apr 1932; **Lady Eileen** Beatrice **Forbes** (1 Jul 1912 - 1993) daughter of Bernard Forbes, 8th Earl of Granard & Beatrice Mills

  A) **Sir John Crichton-Stuart KBE, 6th Marquess of Bute**, etc. (27 Feb 1933 London – 22 Jul 1993 Mount Stuart) (twin) suc. father as Marquess 14 Aug 1956
=1 19 Apr 1955 London (dv.1977); Beatrice **Nicole** Grace **Weld-Forester** (*19 Nov 1933) daughter of Wolstan Weld-Forester & Anne Home-Douglas-Moray
=2 12 Nov 1978; **Jennifer Home-Rigg** (…) =1st Gerald Percy
issue of 1st:
  1) **Lady Sophia** Anne **Crichton-Stuart** (*27 Feb 1956)
=1 23 Jun 1979 London (dv.1988); **James** Stewart **Bain** (…) son of Alistair Bain
=2 1990; **Alexius** John Benedict **Fenwick** (*1959 London) son of David Fenwick & Susan Heber-Percy; =1st Briony Gyngell
issue of 1st:
    a) **Samantha** Ella **Bain** (*25 Jun 1981)
issue of 2nd:
    b) **Georgia** Jessie **Fenwick** (*Aug 1990 London)
  2) **Lady** Eileen **Caroline Crichton-Stuart** (21 Feb 1957 – 1984 Cranwell, Lincolnshire) killed in a car crash
  3) **John** Colum **Crichton-Stuart, 7th Marquess of Bute**

etc.(*26 Apr 1958) suc.father as Marquess 22 Jul 1993
=1 1984 (dv.1993); **Carolyn Waddell** (…) daughter of Bryson Waddell
=2 13 Feb 1999; **Serena** Solitaire **Wendell** (*1960 London) daughter of Jack Wendell & Anthea Hyslop; she =1st Robert De Lisser
issue of 1st:
  a) **Lady Caroline Crichton-Stuart** (*26 Sep 1984 London)
  b) **Lady Cathleen Crichton-Stuart** (*14 Sep 1986)
  c) **John** Bryson, **Earl of Dumfries** (*21 Dec 1989)
issue of 2nd:
  d) **Lady Lola** Affrica **Crichton-Stuart** (*23 Jun 1999 London)
 4) **Lord Anthony Crichton-Stuart** (*14 May 1961)
  = 8 Sep 1990 Great Snoring, Norfolk; **Alison Bruce** (…) daughter of Keith Bruce
  a) **Flora** Grace **Crichton-Stuart** (*10 Nov 1994 New York)
  b) **Eliza** Rose **Crichton-Stuart** (*7 Mar 1996 New York)
  c) **Arthur** Alec **Crichton-Stuart** (*23 Jan 2001 New York City)

B) **Lord David** Ogden **Crichton-Stuart** (27 Feb 1933 London - 1977) (twin)
= 24 Feb 1972; **Helen McColl** (…) daughter of William McColl
 1) **Elizabeth** Rose **Crichton-Stuart** (*10 Mar 1973)
 2) **Kenneth** Edward David **Crichton-Stuart** (*27 Jun 1975)
  = 27 Aug 2005 London; **Kaye Smith** (…) daughter of George Smith
  a) **Georgina** Elizabeth Helen **Crichton-Stuart** (*29 Sep 2010)

C) **Lord James** Charles **Crichton-Stuart** (17 Sep 1935 – 5 Dec 1982 Upton Grey, Hampshire)
=1 25 Jun 1959 London (dv.1968); **Sarah** Frances **Croker-Poole** (*28 Jan 1940 New Delhi, India) daughter of Arthur Poole; =2nd Karim IV, Aga Khan
=2 1970 London; **Anna-Rose Bramwell** (…) daughter of Henry Bramwell; =2nd Peter Knatchbull-Hugessen

issue of 2nd: (none by 1st):
1) **William** Henry **Crichton-Stuart** (*2 Jan 1971 London)
= 2009; **Susan Daniels** (...) daughter of Robert Daniels & Claire ...
no issue
2) **Hugh** Bertram **Crichton-Stuart** (*20 Mar 1973 London)
= 11 Sep 1999 Paarl, South Africa; **Kerry-Anne Reid** (...) daughter of Leo Reid
   a) **Philippa** Jane **Crichton-Stuart** (*16 Oct 1999 Capetown, South Africa)
   b) **Katharine** Morgan **Crichton-Stuart** (*28 May 2003 Capetown)
3) **Alexander** Blain **Crichton-Stuart** (*26 Apr 1982 London)
= 2007; **Susannah Collett** (*Jun 1984 London) daughter of Alan Collett & ... Bennett
issue ?
D) **Lady** Caroline Moira Fiona **Crichton-Stuart** (*7 Jan 1941)
= 4 May 1959; **Michael Lowsley-Williams** (...) son of Francis Lowsley-Williams & Monica Makins
1) **Patrick** David Edward **Lowsley-Williams** (*10 Feb 1960)
2) **Mark** Ogden Francis **Lowsley-Williams** (*26 Feb 1961 London)
3) **Paul** John Fermin **Lowsley-Williams** (*22 Mar 1964 London)
= 27 Jun 1992 Orleans, Massachusetts; **Elizabeth** Compton **Allyn** (...) daughter of Rev. Compton Allyn & Elizabeth ...
4) **Michael** Charles Javier **Lowsley-Williams** (*... 1967)
III) **Lady Jean Crichton-Stuart** (28 Oct 1908 Edinburgh – 23 Oct 1995 Rome)
= 12 Jun 1928; **Hon. James** Willoughby **Bertie** (22 Sep 1901 – 11 May 1966 Malta) son of Montagu Bertie, 7th Earl of Abingdon & Gwendoline Dormer
A) **Fra Andrew** Willoughby Ninian **Bertie, 78th Grand Master of the Sovereign Order of Malta** (15 May 1929 London – 7 Feb 2008 Rome) elected Grand Master 8 Apr 1988

B) Charles **Peregrine** Albemarle **Bertie** (*2 Jan 1932 London)
= 20 Apr 1960 London; **Susan** Giselda Anne Lyon **Wills** (*8 Apr 1940 London) daughter of John Wills & Hon. Jean Elphinstone
  1) **David** Montagu Albemarle **Bertie** (*12.2.1963 Windsor)
    = 12 Feb 1994 Burton-on-Kendal; **Catherine** Cecily **Mason-Hornby** (*7 May 1964) daughter of Antony Mason-Hornby & Cecily Carter
    a) **Charlotte** Iona Rose **Bertie** (*27 Mar 1995 Windor)
    b) **Lucy** Victoria Isabella **Bertie** (*5 Feb 1998 Windsor)
    c) **Hugo** Peregrine Anthony **Bertie** (*18 May 2001 Windsor)
    d) **Rory** Willoughby James **Bertie** (*9 Sep 2003 Windsor)
  2) **Caroline** Georgina Rose **Bertie** (*6 Mar 1965)
    = 3 Sep 1991 Tattendon, Berkshire; **Andrew Carrington** (*5 Dec 1959) son of Norman Carrington & Caroline Campbell
    a) **Georgia** Elizabeth Jean **Carrington** (*9 Jul 1994 Bath)
    b) **Charles** Alexander Francis **Carrington** (*27 Jul 1996 Bath)
IV) **Lord Robert Crichton-Stuart** (12 Dec 1909 - 1976)
= 18 Apr 1934 Windsor; **Lady Janet** Egidia **Montgomerie** (13 May 1911 – 30 Dec 1999) daughter of Archibald Montgomerie, 16th Earl of Eglinton and Winton & Lady Beatrice Dalrymple
  A) **Ninian Crichton-Stuart** (31 Oct 1935 London - 1992)
  B) **Henry** Colum **Crichton-Stuart** (*1 Apr 1938 London)
    = 20 Jul 1963 (dv.1985); **Patricia** Margaret **Norman** (*27 May 1940) daughter of Hugh Norman & Margaret Griffin; she =2nd Robert Kindersley
    1) **Camilla Crichton-Stuart** (*15 Apr 1964)
      = Dec 1994; Martin **Andreas Carleton-Smith** (*1967) son of Sir Michael Carleton-Smith & Helga Stoss
      a) **Joshua** Michael **Carleton-Smith** (*1998)
      b) **Katinka Carleton-Smith** (*2000)
    2) **Serena Crichton-Stuart** (*9 Jul 1965)
      = 1993; **Morgan** Jonathan **Watts** (…) daughter of Dennis Watts
      a) **Megan** Isabella **Watts** (*May 1994 London)
      b) **Lily** Eve **Watts** (*Jun 1997)

3) **Alexander** Colum **Crichton-Stuart** (*4 Feb 1967 London)
= 2001; **Isabella Martin** (…)
issue ?
4) **Teresa** Clare **Crichton-Stuart** (*1971 London)
= 1995; **Toby Mermagen** (…)
   a) **Sam** Timothy **Mermagen** (*Sep 1999)
   b) **Jake** Henry **Mermagen** (*Nov 2001)
   c) **Ella** Jean **Mermagen** (*Jun 2004)

V) **Lord David Stuart** (8 Feb 1911 - 1970) discontinued use of Crichton 1934
= 24 May 1940 Edinburgh; **Ursula** Sybil Clifton **Packe** (2 Feb 1913 - 1989) daughter of Sir Edward Packe & Hon. Mary Colebrooke; =1st Peter Clifton
A) **Flora Stuart** (3 Aug 1941 Isle of Bute – 27 Feb 2005)
B) **Rose Stuart** (6 Apr 1946 – 5 Jan 1962) killed in a car crash

VI) **Lord Patrick Crichton-Stuart** (1 Feb 1913 - 5 Feb 1956)
=1 14 Oct 1937 London; **Jane von Bahr** (… - 18 Dec 1944 Stockholm)
=2 16 Apr 1947; **Linda** Irene **Evans** (16 Apr 1922 - 1974 London) daughter of William Evan
issue of 1st (none by 2nd):
A) **Charles** Patrick Colum Henrey **Crichton-Stuart** (10 Mar 1939 – 3 Jul 2001)
=1 7 Jul 1967 London (dv.); **Shirley Anne Field** (*27 Jun 1938 Bolton, Lancashire) née Broomfield; was raised in an orphanage; took name Field as an actress
=2 1980; **Jennifer A Collie** (*1959)
issue of 1st:
1) **Nicola** Jane **Crichton-Stuart** (*1967 London)
   = Apr 1994 London; **Stuart Gill** (…)
   a) **Charlie Gill** (*Sep 1998 London)
   b) **Max Gill** (*Mar 2001 London)
issue of 2nd:
2) **Sophie Crichton-Stuart** (*1980 London)
3) **Patrick** James **Crichton-Stuart** (*1982 Oxford)
B) **Angela** Mary Monica **Crichton-Stuart** (*25 Mar 1940)
= 19 Feb 1963 London (dv.); **Simon** Mark **Pilkington** (1938 London - 25 Mar 2009) son of Mark Pilkington & Susan Henderson; =2nd Caroline Ramsay
1) **Rupert** Charles **Pilkington** (*21 Feb 1964 London)
2) **Mark** Patrick **Pilkington** (*6 Oct 1965 London)

    = 1999; **Gaynor Driscoll** (…)
     a) **Iain Pilkington** (*2004)
  3) **Jane** Susan **Pilkington** (*7 Nov 1966)
    = 1996; **Brett Marshall** (…) son of Stanley Marshall
     a) **India** Rose **Marshall** (*2001)
     b) **Amber Marshall** (...)
  4) **Kate** Susan **Pilkington** (*23 May 1970 Ayr)
    = 24 Sep 2004; **Tom Shepherd** (...)
     a) **Amelie** Janey McEwen **Shepherd** (*2005)
     b) **Isla** Monique Curzon **Shepherd** (*2007)
VII) **Lord Rhidian Crichton-Stuart** (4 Jun 1917 Cardiff – 25 Jun 1969 London)
= 20 Jul 1939 London; **Selina Gerthe van Wijk** (24 Apr 1913 – 4 May 1985) daughter of Fredrik van Wijk & Charlotte de Casarotto
 A) **Fredrik** John Patrick **Crichton-Stuart** (6 Sep 1940 - 14 Jun 2011 Edinburgh)
  = 3 Oct 1964 London; **Elizabeth** Jane Douglas **Whitson** (*3 Mar 1944) daughter of Ernest Whitson & Jean Miller
  1) **Ione** Jane **Crichton-Stuart** (*22 Nov 1965)
    = 2005; **Collin Tulloch** (...)
  2) **Rhidian** Colum **Crichton-Stuart** (*3 Aug 1967)
    = 16 Sep 1997; **Claire Stead** (…)
     a) **Isabelle** Alexandra **Crichton-Stuart** (*2 Feb 1997 London)
  3) **Amanda** Mary **Crichton-Stuart** (*31 Oct 1968)
  4) **Alexandra** Victoria **Crichton-Stuart** (12 Jul 1973 – 5 Jun 1978)
  5) **Edward** James Neil **Crichton-Stuart** (*27 Dec 1974)
 B) Mary **Margot** Patricia **Crichton-Stuart** (*18 Mar 1942)
  = 20 Jun 1962; **Edward** Henry **Lovell** (…)
  1) **Nicola** Mary **Lovell** (*23 Aug 1963 London)
    = 1983 (dv.); **Francis Maxwell of Kirkconnel** (…)
     a) **Georgia Maxwell** (…)
     b) **Bettina Maxwell** (…)
     c) **Clementina Maxwell** (…)
     d) **Merlin Maxwell** (…)
     e) **Robert Maxwell** (…)
  2) **Peter** Henry James **Lovell** (*21 Feb 1965)
    = 1988; **Nicola Fazakerley** (…)
     a) **James** Alexander **Lovell** (*1990)

      b) **Alexander** Hugh **Lovell** (*1993)
    3) **Henrietta** Margaret **Lovell** (*1971)
  C) Jerome **Niall** Anthony **Crichton-Stuart** (*1 Jan 1948)
  = 1971 London; **Susan Dwyer-Joyce** (…) daughter of Patrick Dwyer-Joyce
    1) Rhidian **Charles** Patrick **Crichton-Stuart** (*1974)
    = 2007; **Olivia** Rosemary **Blomfield-Smith** (*1976) daughter of Clive Blomfield-Smith & Eirenice Gore-Booth
    no issue
    2) Niall **Rollo** Robert **Crichton-Stuart** (*1977)
    = Sep 2005 London; **Eun-Lee Isobella** Gage **Heygate** (*1977) daughter of Sir Richard Heygate, 6th Baronet & Jong-Ja Hyun
      a) **Henry** Richard Niall **Crichton-Stuart** (*20 Jan 2010)
    3) **Archie** Michael John **Crichton-Stuart** (*Jan 1984 London)

d. **Roger** Charles Noel **Bellingham** (28 Apr 1884 Oakham, Sussex – 4 Mar 1915 Flanders, Belgium) killed in action
= 18 Jan 1910 Brighton, Sussex; **Alice** Maud **Naish** (1878 - 10 Jan 1949)
  I) **Sir Roger** Carroll Patrick Stephen **Bellingham, 6th Baronet** (23 Aug 1911 – 6 Feb 1973 Stockport, Cheshire) suc. uncle as Baronet 19 May 1956
  = 27 Dec 1941; **Mary Norman** (…) daughter of William Norman
    A) **Sir Noel** Peter Roger **Bellingham, 7th Baronet** (4 Sep 1943 – 12 Jul 1999) suc. father as Baronet 6 Feb 1973
    = 1977; **Jane Taylor** (…) daughter of Edwin Taylor
    no issue
    B) **Sir Anthony** Edward Norman **Bellingham, 8th Baronet** (*24 Mar 1947 Stockport) suc. brother as Baronet 12 Jul 1999
    =1 16 Feb 1990 Santa Barbara, California (dv.1998); **Denise** Marie **Moity** (*22 Feb 1954 New Orleans, Louisiana) daughter of Henry Moity & …
    =2 … (dv.); **Namphon Buchar** (…)
    issue of 1st (none by 2nd):
      1) **William** Alexander Noel Henry **Bellingham** (*19 Aug 1991) heir-apparent to Baronetcy
  II) **Constance** Catherine Mary Pia **Bellingham** (21 Oct 1912 – …)
  =1 23 Apr 1935; **Brenden Russell** (… - 23 Jun 1956) son of

Charles Russell
=2 7 Jan 1963; Robert **Oswald** H. **Shaw-Hamilton** (1904 Suffolk - ...) son of Robert Shaw-Hamilton
issue of 1st (none by 2nd):
  A) **Heber Russell** (*1936)
    = 1961; **Cora** Ann **Walsh** (...)
    1) **Nigel** Brenden Charles **Russell** (*1962)
    2) **Hilary** Elizabeth Ann **Russell** (*... 1965)
  B) **Una Russell** (*1939) (twin)
    = 1965; **Patrick** Rory **White** (...)
    1) **Sharon** Ann **White** (*1966)
  C) **Anne** M **Russell** (*1939) (twin)
    = 1967; **Charles** W **Fyson** (...)
    1) **Erik** Christopher **Fyson** (*1969)
  D) **Patrick Russell** (*1942)
    = 1966; **Carol** Ann **Banbrook** (*1943) daughter of Henry Banbrook & Dorothy Potts
    1) **Brendan** Daniel **Russell** (*1967)
    2) **Nicholas** Damian **Russell** (*1968)
3. **Sister Edith** Horatia Emma Frances **Noel** (1849 - 22 Aug 1890 London)
4. **Sir Charles** William Francis **Noel, 3rd Earl of Gainsborough** etc. (20 Oct 1850 Campden House, Chipping Camden, Gloucestershire – 17 Apr 1926 Campden House) suc. father as Earl 13 Aug 1881
=1 9 May 1876 Pershore, Hereford; **Augusta** Mary Catherine **Berkeley** (18 Mar 1852 Spetchley, Worcestershire – 5 Nov 1877 Spetchley) daughter of Robert Berkeley & Lady Mary Brown
=2 2 Feb 1880 in Ireland; **Mary Elizabeth Dease** (1858 Turbotston, Westmeath, Ireland – 17 Nov 1937) daughter of James Dease & Charlotte Jerningham
issue of 1st:
  a. **Lady Agnes** Mary Catherine **Noel** (9 Oct 1877 Spetchley – 1 Mar 1915 Oakham)
  issue of 2nd:
  b. **Lady Norah** Ida Emily **Noel** (4 Jan 1881 Campden House – 23 May 1939 Brighton)

= 8 Sep 1915 Exton; **Count Robert** Charles **Bentinck**[12] (5 Dec 1875 London – 12 Mar 1932 Ashwell, Hertfordshire) son of Count Henry Bentinck & Harriett McKerrel
I) **Countess Brydgytte** Blanche **Bentinck** (11 Nov 1916 Bristol – 5 Sep 2010 Haren, Netherlands)
= 2 Feb 1937 London; **Jonkheer**[13] **Adriaan** Hendrik Sibble **van der Wyck** (22 Jun 1906 The Hague – 4 Nov 1973 Haren) son of Jonkheer Evret vand der Wyck
  A) **Caroline** Norah Frederique Adrienne **van der Wyck** (*1 Jun 1938)
    = May 1961; Karel Jan **André** Guyon, **Baron Collot d'Escury** (12 Jul 1933 Kloosterzande - 17 Jun 2008 Kloosterzande) son of Henrik, Baron Collot d'Escury & Juliette Vogelvanger
    1) **Guyon** Adolf Andre **Collot d'Escury** (*25 Apr 1962)
    2) **Juliette** Brygytte Blanche **Collot d'Escury** (*12 Aug 1963)
    3) **Marina** Caroline Norah **Collot d'Escury** (*30 Mar 1965)
      = 1992; **Christaan Bellaar Spruyt** (*1964)
      a) **Nora Bellaar Spruyt** (*1999)
      b) **Anneke Bellaar Spruyt** (*2001)
      c) **Andre Bellaar Spruyt** (*2002)
    4) Robert **Willem** Frederick **Collot d'Escury** (*1970)
      = ...; **Caroline Gockel** (...)
  B) Brydgytte Agnes **Dawn van der Wyck** (*6 Jan 1940)
    = 2 Mar 1968 (dv.1990); **Paul** Heinz Maria Dirk **Vermeer** (*1935)
    1) **Robert** Paul Adriaan Henry Simon **Vermeer** (*14 Oct 1968)
      issue by **Mirielle Brasz** (…):
      a) **Romy Vermeer** (*2004)
      b) **Amy Vermeer** (*18 Mar 2006)
    2) **Fiona** Victoria Regina Brydgytte **Vermeer** (*1970)
    3) **Nadia** Norah Noel **Vermeer** (*1971)
      issue by **Bert-Jan Waanders** (*1967):
      a) **Joep Waanders** (*2002)
      b) **Norah Waanders** (*2007)
  C) **Raina** Jeanne Woltera **van der Wyck** (*2 Dec 1942)
    = 1973; **Hendryk van Harrenfeld** (…)

---

[12] This branch of the Bentinck family was granted the title of Count by the Holy Roman Emperor in 1742. Queen Victoria granted the family permission to continue to carry the title in 1886 as British subjects.
[13] Jonkheer is a Dutch style of nobility that does not have an English translation.

1) **Hugo** Johannes Hendrik **van Harrenfeld** (*1974)
   2) **Wendela** Blanche Catheriune **van Harrenfeld** (*1977)
   3) **Diederik** Godard Adriaan Roelant **van Harrenfeld** (*1980)
  D) **Jonkheer Evert** Rein Robert Henry **van der Wyck** (*12 Aug 1945)
   = 1967; **Tanja Wolff** (*1944)
   1) **Rhoderick** Wolter Arnold **van der Wyck** (*20 Apr 1968 Capetown, S.Africa)
    = 9 Nov 2002 Voorschoten, Netherlands (civil) & 9 Nov 2002 Braschaar, Belgium (rel); **Emily** Anna Hubertina Maria **Bremers** (*1970 Groesbeek, Belgium) daughter of Louis Bremers & Lisanne Rottier
     a) **Philip** Rein Lodewijk **van der Wyck** (*17 Jun 2003 The Hague)
     b) **Maurits** Rhoderick August **van der Wyck** (*5 Aug 2004 The Hague)
   2) **Arnaud van der Wyck** (*1969)
    = Jun 2004 Voorschoten; **Anouk …** (…)
    issue ?
   3) **Alexander van der Wyck** (*… 1971)
    = 8 (civil) & 15 (rel) Dec 2001 Voorschoten;
    Stephanie Carlier (…)
     a) **Gwendolyn van der Wyck** (*20 Jul 2003 The Hague)
     b) **Felicia** Stephanie Elizabeth **van der Wyck** (*20 Oct 2004 The Hague)
  E) **Jonkheer Douglas** Roderick Arthur Duncan **van der Wyck** (*9 May 1955)
II) **Henry** Noel **Bentinck, 11th Earl of Portland,** Viscount Woodstock, Baron Cirencester, **Count Bentinck** (2 Oct 1919 London – 30 Jan 1997 Little Cudworthy, Devon) suc. cousin as Count Bentinck 4 Aug 1968; suc. the 9th Duke of Portland as Earl etc.31 Jul 1990
 =1 13 Oct 1972 London; **Pauline Mellowes** (15 Oct 1921 London – 10 Jan 1967 Potten End, Hertfordshire) daughter of Frederick Mellowes & Doris Watts
 =2 23 Feb 1974 Nettleden, Hertfordshire; **Jenifer Hopkins** (*13 May 1936 London) daughter of Reginald Hopkins & Nancy Page
 issue of 1st (none by 2nd):

A) **Lady Sorrel** Deirdre **Bentinck**[14] (*22 Feb 1942 Selborne, Hampshire) resumed maiden name 1990
= 24 Jun 1972 Nettleden (dv.1988); **Sir John** Philip **Lister-Kaye, 8th Baronet** (*8 May 1946 Wakefield, Yorkshire) son of Sir John Lister-Kaye, 7th Baronet & Audrey Carter; =2nd Lucinda Law; suc.father as Baronet 1982
  1) John **Warwick** Noel **Lister-Kaye** (*10 Dec 1974 Inverness, Scotland) heir-apparent to Baronetcy
  2) **Melanie** Helen **Lister-Kaye** (*12 Oct 1976 Inverness) (twin)
    = 4 Nov 2000 Inverness; David **Ieuan** Picton **Evans** (*22 Mar 1975 Sawnsea, Wales) son of Alan Evans & Mary Harries
    a) **Harris** Ifan Picton **Evans** (*16 Dec 2008)
    b) due 2011
  3) **Amelia** Helen **Lister-Kaye** (*12 Oct 1976 Inverness) (twin)
    = 11 Oct 2008 Camabridge; **Andrew** Colin **Williamson** (*6 Mar 1970 London)
    a) **Arthur** Leonard Jupiter Lister **Williamson** (*8 Aug 2008 Cambridge)
    b) **Elisabeth** Lily Bo Sorrel **Williamson** (*9 Sep 2009 Cambridge)
B) **Lady Anna** Cecilia **Bentinck** (*18 May 1947 Selborne) retained her maiden name
=1 24 Jul 1965 Berkhamstead, Herfordshire (dv.1974); **Jasper** Hamilton **Holmes** (*14 Nov 1941 Hartford, Cheshire)
=2 19 Jul 1975 London (dv.1977); **Nicholas** George Spafford **Vester** (*30 Mar 1944 Cambridge)
no issue by marriages
issue by **Arnold** George Francis **Cragg** (*30 Sep 1943) son of Rt. Rev. Kenneth Cragg:
  1) **Gulliver** Jack Bentinck **Cragg** (*1 Jul 1978 London)
  2) **George** Finn Gareth Bentinck **Cragg** (*4 Oct 1980 London)
  3) **Iris Cragg** (* & + 15 Jul 1986 London) (twin)
  4) **Pierre Cragg** (* & + 15 Jul 1986 London) (twin)
  5) **Charlotte-Sophie** Camden Bentinck **Cragg** (*29 Mar

---

[14] Although entitled to by styled Count or Countess Bentinck, the children of the Earls of Portland have chosen to be known only by their British styles.

C) **Timothy** Charles Robert Noel **Bentinck, 12th Earl of Portland** etc, **Count Bentinck** (*1 Jun 1953 in Tasmania) suc.father as Earl and Count 30 Jan 1997
  = 8 Sep 1979 London; **Judith** Ann **Emerson** (*10 Oct 1952 Newcastle-under-Lyme) daughter of John Emerson & Mary Graham
  1) **William** Jack Henry, **Viscount Woodstock** (*19 May 1984 London)
  2) **Hon. Jasper** James Mellowes **Bentinck** (*12 Jun 1988 London)

c. **Sir Arthur** Edward Joseph **Noel, 4th Earl of Gainsborough** etc. (30 Jun 1884 Exton Park – 27 Aug 1927 Exton Park) suc. father as Earl 17 Apr 1926
= 10 Nov 1915; **Alice** Mary **Eyre** (17 Oct 1886 Lima, Peru – 11 Jun 1970 London) daughter of Edward Eyre & Elisa Ainsworth
  I) **Lady Maureen** Therese Josephine **Noel** (7 Mar 1917 London - 25 Nov 2009 Chipping Camden, Gloucestershire)
  =1 19 Feb 1944 London; **Sir Charles** Walter James **Dormer, 15th Baron Dormer, 15th Baronet** (20 Dec 1903 Malta – 27 Aug 1975 London) son of Sir Charles Dormer, 14th Baron Dormer & Caroline Clifford; suc.father as Baron 4 May 1922
  =2 22 Jul 1982; **Peregrine** Edward Lancelot **Fellowes** (8 Jul 1912 Calgary, Alberta – 15 Feb 1999 Chipping Camden) son of Henry Fellowes & Georgina Wrightson; =1st Olwen Stuart-Jones
  issue of 1st (none by 2nd):
  A) **Hon. Jane** Maureen Therese **Dormer** (*20 Nov 1945 London)
  =1 21 Jul 1966 London (dv.1978); Henry Alistair **Samuel Sandbach** (*1944) son of Ralph Sandbach
  =2 1980 London; **Geoffrey** Edward **Meek** (1921 - Mar 1984)
  =3 Jan 1988 London; **Robert** Nigel Forbes **Glennie** (…)
  issue of 1st (none by others):
  1) **Emma** Pauline Jane **Sandbach** (*29 Jun 1967)
    = May 1993; **Graham** Anthony **Defries** (*1972) son of Nicholas Defries
    a) **Charles** Samuel Nicholas **Defries** (*Feb 1996 London)
    b) **Elisa** Jane Catherine **Defries** (*Apr 1999 London)
    c) **Lara** Betty Maureen **Defreis** (*May 2001 London)
    d) **Arthur** Joseph Graham **Defries** (*Nov 2004 London)

    2) **James** Peter Charles **Sandbach** (*1969 London)
  B) **Hon. Catherine** Mary **Dormer** (*2 Apr 1950 London)
    =1 14 Feb 1973 London (dv.1989); **Christopher** John Godfrey **Bird** (*1946) son of Garth Bird & Elizabeth Vavasour
    =2 May 1992; **Simon** Michael **Stone** (…)
    issue of 2nd: (none by 1st):
    1) **Raphael** Charles **Stone** (*Dec 1992 London)
II) **Sir Anthony** Edward Gerald **Noel, 5th Earl of Gainsborough** etc.(24 Oct 1923 London – 29 Dec 2009 Exton Park) suc.father as Earl 27 Aug 1927
= 23 Jul 1947; **Mary Stourton** (*24 Sep 1925) daughter of Hon. John Stourton & Kathleen Gunther
  A) **Lady Juliana** Mary Alice **Noel** (*27 Jan 1949 Barham Court, Rutland) has resumed maiden name
    = 29 Jan 1970 London (dv.2001); **Edward** Peter Bertram Savile **Foljambe, 5th Earl of Liverpool**, Viscount Hawkesbury, Baron Hawkesbury (*ph.14 Jan 1944) son of Peter Foljambe & Elizabeth Gibbs; suc.grand-uncle as Earl 13 Mar 1969; =2nd Marie Michel de Pierredon; =3rd Georgina Rubin
    1) **Luke** Marmaduke Peter Savile, **Viscount Hawkesbury** (*25 Mar 1972)
    2) **Hon. Ralph** Edward Anthony Savile **Foljambe** (*24 Sep 1974 London)
      = Oct 2003; **Rebecca Parker** (…) daughter of Gordon Parker
      a) **Jemima** Fleur **Foljambe** (*6 Mar 2005)
      b) **Arthur Foljambe** (*2006)
      c) **Hector** George Jocelyn Savile **Foljambe** (*22 Dec 2009)
  B) **Anthony** Baptist **Noel, 6th Earl of Gainsborough** etc. (*16 Jan 1950 Barham Court) suc.father as Earl 29 Dec 2009
    = 23 May 1972 London; **Sarah** Rose **Winnington** (*29 Apr 1951 London) daughter of Thomas Winnington & Lady Betty Anson
    1) **Henry** Robert Anthony, **Viscount Campden** (*1 Jul 1977)
      = Sep 2005 London; **Zara van Cutsem** (*Dec 1978) daughter of Geoffrey van Cutsem & Sally McCorquodale
      a) **Hon. Edward** Patrick Anthony **Noel** (*30 Apr

2007)
   b) **Hon. Violet** Ruth **Noel** (*12 Nov 2009)
C) **Lady Maria Noel** (*3 Feb 1951 Barham Court)
  = 17 Apr 1971; **Robert** D **Pridden** (*1945 Exton, Rutland) son of John Pridden & Ivy Ewin
  1) **Benedict** John Anthony **Pridden** (*23 Sep 1973 London)
     = May 2005; **Georgina** Rose Alianore **Lethbridge** (*1980) daughter of Sir Thomas Lethbridge, 7th Baronet & Susan Rock
     a) **Charlotte** Susan Mary **Pridden** (*8 Nov 2006 York)
     b) **Agatha** Maria Rachael **Pridden** (*4 Apr 2008 Scarborough)
     c) **Robert** Ralph Baptist **Pridden** (*29 Aug 2009 Scarborough)
  2) **Lucy** Charlotte Ivy **Pridden** (*15 Jun 1976 London)
     = 15 Jul 2006 Exton Park; **Piers** Mark **Woodnutt** (*28 Mar 1977 London) son of Martin Woodnutt & Susannah Harrison
     a) **Jack** Robert Mark **Woodnutt** (*31 Jan 2008 London)
     b) due 2011
D) **Lady Janet Noel** (* & + 23 Jan 1953 Barham Court)
E) **Lady Celestria** Magdalena Mary **Noel** (*27 Jan 1954 Exton Park, Rutland)
  = 1 Mar 1990 London; **Timothy Hales** (*2 Apr 1933 London) son of William Hales & Katherine Johnston
  1) **Catherine** Rose Mary **Hales** (*11 Jun 1990 London)
F) **Hon. Gerard** Edward Joseph **Noel** (*23 Jan 1955 Exton Park)
  = 1985; **Charlotte Dugdale** (*15 May 1955) daughter of Sir William Dugdale, 2nd Baronet & Lady Belinda Peydell-Bouverie
  1) **Belinda** Mary **Noel** (*Jul 1986)
  2) Francis **Reginald Noel** (*Jul 1987)
  3) **Lettice** Catherine **Noel** (*Dec 1989)
G) **Hon. Thomas Noel** (*9 Mar 1958 Exton Park)
H) **Hon. Edward** Andrew **Noel** (*22 Nov 1960 Exton Park)
  =1 1990 (dv.1994); **Lavinia** Jane **Bingham** (…) daughter of George Bingham
  =2 19 Jul 1997; **Sarah** Kate **Yeats-Brown** (*9 Jul 1961

London) daughter of David Yeats-Brown & Annesley Eden
issue of 2nd (none 1st):
  1) **Joseph** David **Noel** (*20 Jan 2000)
  III) **Hon. Gerard** Eyre Wriothesley **Noel** (*20 Nov 1926 London)
= 1 Feb 1958 London; **Adele** Julie Patricia **Were** (…) daughter of Bonville Were
  A) **Philip** Arthur Nicholas **Noel** (*26 May 1959)
  B) **Robert** John Baptist **Noel** (*15 Oct 1962)
  C) **Elizabeth** Alice Mary **Noel** (*24 Sep 1967)
= 28 Sep 1996; **Henry** John **Pittman** (…) son of Hugh Pittman & Rosemary Dickinson[15]
  1) **Luke** Nicholas **Pittman** (*6 Jan 1999)
  2) **Marina Pittman** (*10 Sep 2001)
d. **Hon. Charles** Hubert Francis **Noel** (22 Oct 1885 Exton Park – 26 Apr 1947 Kinross, Scotland)
= 31 Jan 1912 London; **May Douglas-Dick** (Jul 1884 London– 1 Apr 1964 London) son of Archibald Douglas-Dick & Isabelle Parrott
  I) **Jane** Isabelle Mary **Noel** (21 Nov 1912 London – 7 Mar 1952 Nunwick, Northumberland)
= 26 Sep 1942 London; **Guy** Hunter **Allgood** (4 Oct 1892 Alnwick, Northumberland – 1 Jun 1970 Nunwick) son of Robert Allgood & Isabel Clayton
  A) Lancelot **Guy Allgood** (1 Feb 1944 Newcastle-upon-Tyne - Jan 1999 Hexham, Northumberland)
= Cirencester; **Veronica Pitman** (*20 Jan 1950 London) daughter of Stuart Pitman & Cynthia …
  1) **Jane** Elizabeth **Allgood** (*3 Apr 1977 Hexham)
= 2008; **James** R **Lamb** (...) son of Robert Lamb
  2) **George** Hunter **Allgood** (1 – 19 May 1979 Hexham)
  3) **Alice** Louise **Allgood** (*14 Aug 1980 Hexham)
  4) **Mary** Rosamund **Allgood** (*21 Feb 1983 Hexham)
= 2010/11; **Henry** H **Lobb** (*1982 Manchester) son of Edward Lobb
  B) **Charles** Noel **Allgood** (*1 May 1945 Corbridge-on-Tyne, Northumberland)

---

[15] Rosemary Dickinson Pittman =2nd Andrew Parker-Bowles, the ex-husband of HRH The Duchess of Cornwall.

C) **James** Major **Allgood** (27 Jun 1948 Nunwick – 15 Mar 1949 Nunwick)
II) **Archibald** Charles William **Noel** (5 Jan 1914 London – 8 Feb 1997)
=1 30 Aug 1945; **Bridget** Mary **Fetherstonbaugh** (26 Dec 1918 – 3 Sep 1976) daughter of William Fetherstonbaugh & Adela Cayley
=2 22 Dec 1977; **Andrée** Marie **Duchen** (…) daughter of Pierre Duchen
issue of 1st (none by 2nd):
A) **Charles** William **Noel** (*4 Jul 1948 Crickhowell)
 = 1985; **Diane** Margaret **de Freitas** (…) daughter of Gerald de Freitas
 1) **Elizabeth** Bridgit Maggie **Noel** (*19 Nov 1986 London)
 2) **Alexander** Charles FitzWilliam **Noel** (*19 Jan 1989 London)
B) **Edward** Albany **Noel** (*28 Sep 1956 Crickhowell)
III) **Carola** Mary **Noel** (3 Jun 1916 London – 19 Mar 1989 Aberfeldy, Scotland)
= 21 Apr 1936 Dundee; **Thomas Steuart Fothringham** (5 Apr 1907 Edinburgh – 9 Sep 1979 Edzell, Scotland) son of Walter Steuart Fothringham & Elizabeth Nicholson
A) **Robert** Scrymsoure **Steuart Fothringham of Pourie**(*5 Aug 1937 Boughton Hall)
 = 16 Feb 1962; **Elizabeth** Mary Charlotte **Lawther** (19 Mar 1938 London - 15 Aug 1990 London) daughter of Thomas Lawther
 1) **Mariana Steuart Fothringham** (*1966)
  = 1 Apr 1989 Murthly, Perthshire; **Christopher** Berkeley **Pease** (27 Apr 1958 London)
  a) **Edward** Robert **Pease** (*7 Jun 1991 London)
  b) **Dorothea** Elizabeth **Pease** (*29 Oct 1992 London)
  c) **Sybilla** Mary **Pease** (*2 Jul 1994 London)
  d) **Carola** Rosemary **Pease** (*19 Feb 1996 London)
 2) **Ilona Steuart Fothringham** (*3 Nov 1969)
  = 30 May 1998 Murthly; **Christopher** Alexander David **Boyle** (…) son of Paul Boyle & Helen …
  a) **George** Alexander David Lindsay **Boyle** (*29 Dec 1999 London)
  b) **Henry** Robert Alfred Lindsay **Boyle** (*1 Apr 2002 London)

c) **Elizabeth** Mary Agatha **Boyle** (*24 Sep 2008 Carlisle)
  3) **Thomas Steuart Fothringham** (*20 Sep 1971)
   = 7 Aug 1999 Murthly; Anna **Catherine Macdonald** (*11 Apr 1969 Melbourne, Australia) daughter of Allan Macdonald & Anthea Poultney
   a) **Alexander** Donald **Steuart Fothringham** (*30 Sep 2001 Edinburgh)
   b) **James** Andrew **Steuart Fothringham** (*17 Nov 2005 Dundee)
  4) **Lionel Steuart Fothringham** (*27 Apr 1973)
   = 2005; **Elizabeth Waller** (…) daughter of David Waller
   a) **Charlotte** Rose **Steuart Fothringham** (*6 Dec 2009)
 B) **Walter Steuart Fothringham** (26 Mar 1939 Edinburgh– 3 Jun 1989 Grantully Castle, Aberfeldy)
  = 8 Jan 1972; **Patricia** Anne **Watherston** (…) daughter of Sir David Watherston
  1) **Teresa** Catherine Frances **Steuart Fothringham** (*22 May 1975)
   = 2005; **Warren Elsmore** (…) son of Malcolm Elsmore issue ?
  2) **David** Frederick **Steuart Fothringham** (*2 Mar 1979)
 C) **Henry Steuart Fothringham** (*15 Feb 1944 Edinburgh)
  = 20 May 1972 Glencreran; **Cherry** Linnhe **Stewart** (25 Jun 1940 Singapore – 17 Dec 2001) daughter of Ian Stewart & Ursula Morley-Fletcher
  1) **Patrick** Donald **Steuart Fothringham** (*23 Apr 1973 Perth, Scotland)
   = 2005; **Suzanna Wilson** (…)
   a) **Hester** Mary **Steuart Fothringham** (*7 Dec 2008)
  2) **Charles** Henry **Steuart Fothringham** (*6 Apr 1974 Perth)
   = 11 Feb 2011 Grandtully, Perthshire; **Sophia MacCarthy-Morrogh** (…) daughter of Alexander MacCarthy-Morrogh
  3) **Ian** Archibald **Steuart Fothringham** (*13 Jan 1976 Perth)
IV) **David** Franics Douglas **Noel** (18 May 1919 London – 2 Jan 1974)
V) **Andrew** Mungo James **Noel** (27 Jul 1921 – 21 Oct 1972)
 = 10 Jan 1950; Mary **Edina Walmesley** (16 Nov 1925 - 13 Jul 2008) daughter of Charles Walmesley & Dorothy Mayne no issue
VI) **Douglas** Robert George **Noel** (*16 Apr 1924 Dundee)
 = 2 Jun 1949 London; **Eleanor** Susan Jane **Younghusband**

(*11 Apr 1928 London) daughter of George Younghusband & Mary Foster
   A) **James** Douglas George **Noel** (*14 Aug 1950 Crickhowell, Wales)
   B) **William** Edward Douglas **Noel** (5 Aug 1953 Crickhowell – 3 Nov 2006)
   =1 19 Jul 1975 London (dv.1982, ann.1984); **Victoria** Mary **Younghusband**[16] (*14 Jul 1954 London) daughter of George Younghusband & Sybil Stuart[17]
   =2 1993; Juliet **Catherine Reade** (…) daughter of Arthur Reade; =1st Henry Hayward
   issue of 1st (none by 2nd):
   1) **Teresa** Sybil **Noel** (*6 Feb 1976 Oxford)
   2) **Arthur** Douglas **Noel** (*6 Oct 1977 London)
      = …; **Marie Bertin** (…)
      a) **Thomas Noel** (*18 Nov 2005)
   C) **Caroline** Mary Jane **Noel** (*6 Jun 1956)
   = 3 Oct 1987 London; **Charles** Anthony **Wentzel** (…) son of John Wentzel & Philippa …
   1) **Philippa** Mary **Wentzel** (*1991)
   e. **Lady Clare** Mary Charlotte **Noel** (3 Mar 1882 Oakham – 11 Mar 1962)
   = 2 Oct 1907 Oakham; **Charles** Mervyn **King** (1878 Clifton, Gloucestershire – 25 Jan 1965 Bristol) son of Mervyn King & Agnes Bright
      I) **Agnes** Celestria Mary **King** (1917 - Oct 2005)
   f. **Hon. Robert** Edmund Thomas More **Noel** (10 Apr 1888 – 2 Feb 1918 Massassi, Zimbabwe) killed in action
5. **Hon. Edward Noel** (28 Apr 1852 Oakham – 9 Nov 1917)
   = 7 Oct 1884 London; **Ruth Lucas** (1852 - Apr 1926)
   a. **Edward** William Charles **Noel** (14 Apr 1886 – 10 Dec 1974)
   =1 6 Apr 1923; **Katherine** Florence **Ross** (1896 – 6 Feb 1952) daughter of Robert Ross
   =2 1954; **Simone Corbiau** (22 Dec 1902 – 27 Oct 1974) daughter of Jean Corbiau
   issue of 1st:
      I) **Rev. Robert** Anthony **Noel** (26 Jan 1924 – 15 Aug 1966)
      II) **Denys** Edward **Noel** (23 Nov 1925 - 1978)

---

[16] William & Victoria are 4th cousins
[17] Sybil is a direct descendant of the 1st Marquess of Bute

= 13 Dec 1947; **Petronelle** Moore **Bostock** (…) daughter of Austin Bostock
A) **Julian** Roden Bostock **Noel** (*5 Jun 1949)
= 1982; **Susanne** Elisabeth **Dodd** (…) daughter of Benjamin Dodd
no issue
B) **Laura** Frances **Noel** (*6 Sep 1951)
= 1979; **Peter** Clement **Coe** (…)
1) **Toby** Richard **Coe** (*1983)
2) **Lucy** Josephine **Coe** (*1985)
3) **Jennifer** Mary **Coe** (*1988)
b. **Hubert** Lewis Clifford **Noel** (19 Oct 1888 Newton Abbott, Devonshire - 1954)
= 25 Aug 1934; **Mary** Maxwell **Currie** (1876 Newcastle-upon-Tyne - 1953) daughter of James Currie & …; =1st Francis Russell
no issue
c. **John** Baptist Lucius **Noel** (26 Feb 1890 – 13 Mar 1989)
=1 1915; **Sybil Graham** (… - 1939)
=2 1941; **Mary Sullivan** (12 Jun 1908 - 1984)
issue of 2nd (none by 1st):
I) **Sandra** Ruth Catherine **Noel** (*15 Apr 1943)
B. **William** Harry **Hay, 19th Earl of Erroll** etc.(3 May 1823 Bushy Park – 3 Dec 1891 Slains Castle, near Cruden, Aberdeenshire) suc. father as Earl 19 Apr 1846
= 20 Sep 1848 Montreal; **Eliza** Amelia **Gore** (24 Feb 1829 Montreal – 11 Mar 1916 London) daughter of Hon. Sir Charles Gore & Lavina FitzRoy
1. **Charles** Gore, **Lord Kilmarnock** (10 – 12 Oct 1850 Slains Castle)
2. **Sir Charles** Gore **Hay KT, 20th Earl of Erroll** etc. (7 Feb 1852 Montreal – 8 Jul 1927) suc. father as Earl 3 Dec 1891; KT 1901
= 11 Aug 1875 Muncaster, Cumberland; **Mary** Caroline **L'Estrange** (May 1849 Tickhill Castle, Yorkshire - 12 Oct 1934) daughter of Edmund L'Estrange & Lady Henrietta Lumley
a. **Sir Victor** Alexander Gerald **Hay, 21st Earl of Erroll** etc. (17 Oct 1876 Slains Castle – 20 Feb 1928) suc. father as Earl 8 Jul 1927
= 22 May 1900 London; Mary **Lucy** Victoria **Mackenzie** (18 Jun 1875 Ness Bank, Inverness- 18 Jan 1957) daughter of Sir Allan Mackenzie, Baronet & Lucy Davidson

I) **Josslyn** Victor **Hay, 22nd Earl of Erroll** etc. (11 May 1901 London – 24 Jan 1941 near Nairobi, Kenya) murdered; suc. father as Earl 20 Feb 1928
=1 22 Sep 1923 (dv.1930); **Lady** Myra **Edina Sackville** (26 Feb 1893 – 5 Nov 1955) daughter of Gilbert Sackville, 8th Earl De La Warr & Lady Muriel Brassey; =1st David Wallace; =2nd Charles Gordon; =4th Donald Haldeman; =5th Vincent Soltau
=2 8 Feb 1930; Edith (**Molly**) Mildred Mary Agnes **Maude** (1893 London - 13 Oct 1939 Happy Valley, Kenya) daughter of Richard Maude; =1st Guy Hunter; =2nd Cyril Ramsay-Hill
issue of 1st (none by 2nd):

A) **Diana** Denyse **Hay, (23rd) Countess of Erroll**, Lady Hay and Slains (5 Jan 1926 Nairobi – 17 May 1978 Oban, Argyll) suc. father as Countess 24 Jan 1941
=1 19 Dec 1946 London (dv.1964); **Sir Robert Iain** Kay **Moncreiffe of that Ilk, 11th Baronet** (9 Apr 1919 – 27 Feb 1985) son of Gerald Moncreiffe of that Ilk & Hilda de Miremont; suc. cousin as Baronet 17 Nov 1957; =2nd Hermoine Falkner
=2 27 Nov 1964 Lonmay; **Raymond** Alexander **Carnegie** (9 Jul 1920 – 6 Sep 1999) son of Hon. Alexander Carnegie & Susan Rodakowski; =1st Patricia Dawson; =3rd Maria Alexander
issue of 1st:

1) **Sir Merlin** Serald Victor Gilbert **Hay, 24th Earl of Erroll** etc[18], **12th Baronet** (*20 Apr 1948 Edinburgh) suc.mother as Earl 17 May 1978; suc.father as Baronet 27 Feb 1985
= 8 May 1982 Winchester, Hampshire; **Isabelle** Jacqueline Laline **Astell** (*22 Aug 1955 Brussels) daughter of Thomas Astell & Jacqueline de Jouffrou d'Abbans; =1st ... Hohler

a) **Harry** Thomas William, **Lord Hay** (*8 Aug 1984 Basingstoke)

b) **Lady Amelia** Diana Jacqueline **Hay** (*23 Sep 1987 Basingstoke)

c) **Lady Laline** Lucy Clementine **Hay** (*21 Dec 1988 Basingstoke)

d) **Hon. Richard** Merlin Ian **Hay** (*14 Dec 1990

---

[18] The Earl of Erroll also serves as the Hereditary Lord High Constable of Scotland. This position gives him precedence before all hereditary Peers and after only the Royal Family in Scotland.

Basingstoke)
2) **Hon. Peregrine** David Euan Malcolm **Moncreiffe of that Ilk** (*16 Feb 1951) recognized as Moncreiffe of that Ilk 11 Jan 2001
= 27 Jul 1988; **Miranda** Mary **Fox-Pitt** (*1968) daughter of Mervyn Fox-Pitt & Janet Wedderburn
   a) **Ossian** Peregrine **Moncreiffe, Younger of that Ilk** (*3 Feb 1991)
   b) **India** Mary **Moncreiffe** (*3 Nov 1992)
   c) **Elizabeth** Miranda Zuri **Moncreiffe** (*2 Feb 1995)
   d) **Alexandra** Hutton Melville **Moncreiffe** (*19 Nov 1996)
   e) **Lily Moncreiffe** (*6 Nov 1998)
   f) **Euan Moncreiffe** (*12 Sep 2000)
3) **Lady Alexandra** Victoria Caroline Anne Hay **Moncreiffe** (*30 Jul 1955 Edinburgh)
= 22 Feb 1989 Perth; **Jocelyn** Christopher Neill **Connell** (*16 May 1952 Perth) son of Christopher Connell & Daphne Wilson
   a) **Flora** Diana Catherine Ceclia **Connell** (*24 Feb 1990 London)
   b) **Ciara** Edith Elizabeth **Connell** (*28 Mar 1994 London) issue by **Sir Michael** Iain **Wigan, 6**[th] **Baronet** (*3 Oct 1951 London) son of Sir Alan Wigan, 5th Baronet & Robina Colquhoun; suc. father as Baronet 3 May 1996:
   c) **Ivar** Francis Grey de Miremont **Wigan** (*25 Mar 1979 Perth)
issue of 2nd:
4) **Hon. Jocelyn** Jacek Alexander **Carnegie** (*21 Nov 1966)
= 1990; **Susie** Mhairi **Butler** (…) daughter of Thomas Butler
   a) **Merlin** Thomas Alexander Bannerman **Carnegie** (*25 Apr 1991)
   b) **Cecilia** Diana Catrina Pearl **Carnegie** (1993 - 1994)
   c) **Maximilian** Archibald Josslyn **Carnegie** (*21 Dec 1995)
   d) **Finn** Kenneth Redvers **Carnegie** (*21 Oct 1997)
   e) **Frederica** Cecilia **Carnegie** (*6 Apr 2000)
   f) **Willa** Cecilia Susan **Carnegie** (*9 Sep 2001)
II) **Gilbert** Allan Rowland **Boyd, 6**[th] **Baron Kilmarnock** (15

Jan 1903 - 15 May 1975 London) suc. brother (Earl of Erroll) as Baron 24 Jan 1941[19] resuming the ancestral name Boyd
=1 12 Jul 1926 (dv.1955); **Hon. Rosemary** Sibell **Guest** (7 Mar 1906 – 21 Mar 1971) daughter of Ivor Guest, 1st Viscount Wimborne & Hon. Alice Grovesnor; =2nd John Berger
=2 17 May 1955; **Denise** Aubrey Doreen **Coker** (1930 - 1989) daughter of Lewis Coker & Doreen Chichester
issue of 1st:

A) **Alistair** Ivor Gilbert **Boyd, 7th Baron Kilmarnock** (11 May 1927 - 19 Mar 2009) suc. father as Baron 15 May 1975
  =1 10 Sep 1954 (dv.1969); **Diana** Mary **Grant Gibson** (30 Sep 1924 – 30 Jun 1975) daughter of Donald Grant Gibson; she =1st ... Hawkins
  =2 18 Feb 1977; **Hilary** Ann **Sidney** (1928 – 24 Jun 2010) daughter of Leonard Sidney & Marjery Bardwell; =1st (later Sir) Kingsley Amis; =2nd Shackleton Bailey
  issue of 2nd (none by 1st):
  1) **Hon. James** Charles Edward **Boyd** (*27 Jan 1972)[20]

B) **Hon. Laura** Alice **Boyd** (10 Jun 1934 London – 25 Feb 1999)
  = 11 Jan 1962 London; Robert **Anthony Hyman** (*3 Apr 1928 London) son of Alexander Hyman & Fanny Rubinstein
  1) **Anthony Hyman** (*27 May 1962 London)
    = ...; **Suzanne Eaton** (...)
    a) **Max Hyman** (*23 Dec 1997)
    b) **Luke Hyman** (*22 Sep 1999)
  2) **Fanny Hyman** (*19 Dec 1963 Kintyre)
    = 26 Mar 1994; **Charles** Richard **Mills** (*26 Jan 1958) son of Kenneth Mills & Jane Pelly
    a) **Samuel** Charles **Mills** (*17 Dec 1995)
    b) **Silvia** Fanny **Mills** (*22 Jul 1997)
    c) **Victor** George **Mills** (*22 May 2001)

---

[19] The Barony of Kilmarnock was created in he Peerage of the United Kingdom which generally does not permit succession by a female unless there is a special remainder included in to the creation. In this case there was not, so while the Countess of Erroll was able to inherit the Scottish titles, the UK title went to the next male.

[20] Being born before his parents' marriage, James is not entitled to inherit the Barony of Kilmarnock

3) **Merlin Hyman** (*10 Sep 1969 London)
   = …; **Katy Vincent** (…)
   a) **Harry Hyman** (*4 Jan 2000)
   b) **Elizabeth** Laura May **Hyman** (*7 Dec 2001)
   c) **Florence Hyman** (*15 Jul 2003)
C) **Juliet Hay** (1 – 2 May 1937) (twin)
D) **Iris Hay** (* & + 1 May 1937) (twin)
E) **Hon. Caroline** Juliet **Boyd** (*31 Jul 1939)
   = 1969 London; **Alan** Thomas **Bloss** (*1938) son of Thomas Bloss & Jane Hodgson
   no issue
F) **Robin** Jordan **Boyd, 8th Baron Kilmarnock** (*6 Jun 1941) suc. brother as Baron 19 Mar 2009
   =1 1977 (dv.1986); **Ruth** Christine **Fisher** (…) daughter of Michael Fisher
   =2 2000; **Hilary** Vivian **Cox** (…) daughter of Peter Cox
   issue of 1st:
   1) **Hon. Simon** John **Boyd** (*1979) heir-apparent to father
      = 2004; **Valeria** Beatriz **Matzkin** (...) daughter of Jorge Matzkin
      a) **Florence** Emilia **Boyd** (*2005)
      b) **Lucien** Michael **Boyd** (*2007)
   2) **Hon. Mark** Julia **Boyd** (*1981)
   issue by **Catherine Hoddell** (…):
   3) **Alice** Rowena **Boyd** (*1989)
   issue of 2nd:
G) **Hon. Jonthan** Aubrey Lewis **Boyd** (*1 Oct 1956 London)
   = 20 Mar 1982; **Annette** Madeleine **Constantine** (*1956 London) daughter of Joseph Constantine & Mary Cotter
   1) **Edward** Gilbert **Boyd** (*14 Mar 1989 London)
   2) **Arthur** William **Boyd** (*11 Dec 1994 London)
H) **Hon. Timothy** Iain **Boyd** (*5 Apr 1959 London)
   = 1988; **Lucy** Teresa Emily **Gray** (…) daughter of Michael Gray
   1) **Daisy Boyd** (*1988)
III) **Lady Rosemary** Constance Ferelith **Hay** (15 May 1904 – 19 May 1944)
   =1 29 May 1924 (dv.1935); **Rupert** Sumner **Ryan** (6 May 1884 Melbourne – 25 Aug 1952 Berwick, Victoria) son of

Sir Charles Ryan & Alice Sumner
=2 27 Jun 1935; **James** Frank **Gresham** (21 Dec 1909 - 1983 Aberconwy) son of Frank Gresham
issue of 1st (none by 2nd):
  A) **Patrick** Victor Charles **Ryan** (5 May 1925 Koblenz, Germany – 15 Jul 1989 Melbourne, Australia)
    = 1949 South Yarra, Victoria, Australia; **Rosemary** Elizabeth **Chesterman** (10 Oct 1927 Hobart, Tasmania – 19 Sep 1996 Victoria) daughter of Francis Chesterman & Thelma Foster
    1) **Dominic** Rupert Charles **Ryan** (*21 May 1956 London)
    2) **Siobhan** Ferelith Fionola **Ryan** (*25 Aug 1959 Melbourne)
      = Mar 1994 South Yarra; **Mark Douglas** (…)
      a) **Hunter Ryan-Douglas** (*12 Mar 1990 Melbourne)
b. **Hon. Serald** Mordaunt Alan Josslyn **Hay** (Nov 1877 – 12 Nov 1939)
= 26 Apr 1915; **Violet Spiller** (…) daughter of Duncan Spiller
no issue
c. **Hon. Ivan** Josslyn Lumley **Hay** (31 Oct 1884 Slains Castle – 6 Sep 1936)
= 8 Nov 1921; **Pamela Burroughes** (Apr 1895 Seal, Kent – 23 Nov 1977) daughter of Francis Burroughes & Abbe Bourke
  I) **Alexandra** Cecilia Mary **Hay** (26 Sep 1922 – 29 Apr 1991 London)
  II) **Elizabeth** Anne **Hay** (3 Feb 1925 - Dec 2005 Birmingham)
    = 20 Oct 1945 London (dv.1970); **Jeremy** Christopher **Gurney** (15 Oct 1925 - Oct 1991 London) son of Christopher Guerney & Joan Grenfell
    A) **Michael** Jeremy **Gurney** (*3 Nov 1946)
      = 14 Feb 1981 London (dv.1997); **Hon.** Diana **Miranda Hovell-Thurlow-Cumming-Bruce** (*6 Jul 1954) daughter of Francis Hovell-Thurlow-Cumming-Bruce, 8th Baron Thurlow & Yvonne Wilson; =2nd Vanya Boestoem
      1) **Rohan** Samphie Katherine **Gurney** (*1981)
      2) **Mungo** James Nicholas **Gurney** (*1982 London)
    B) **William** Ivan **Gurney** (*23 Mar 1948)
      = 10 Aug 1973; **Annette** Marie **Deutsch** (*6 Jan 1949 Limerick) daughter of Robert Deutsch & Elizabeth …
      1) **Stella** Elizabeth **Gurney** (*1975 Birmingham)
        = Jul 2003 London; **Mark Griffiths** (...)
      2) **Luke Gurney** (* & +1977 Birmingham)

   3) **Leo** Robert Ivan **Gurney** (*1978 Birmingham)
    = ...; **Kate** Rose **Hall** (*19 Oct 1978 London) daughter of
    Dave Hall & Wendy ...
    a) **Rosa Guerney** (*11.4.2010 Newcastle)
  III) **Penelope** Constance Lumley **Hay** (*26 Mar 1930)
   = 25 May 1957; **George** Harold Armine **Dare** (2 Nov
   1918 - 13 Mar 2010) son of Harold Dare & Sibyl Morriss
   A) **Henry** James **Dare** (*3 Mar 1959)
   B) **Amelia** Alexandra Elizabeth **Dare** (*27 Nov 1961
   London)
 3. **Hon. Arthur Hay** (16 Sep 1855 Slains Castle – 1 May 1932)
 4. **Lady Florence** Alice **Hay** (28 May 1858 Slains Castle – 15 May 1859 Slains Castle)
 5. **Lady Cecilia** Leila **Hay** (4 Mar 1860 – 7 Jan 1925)
  = 31 Oct 1883 London; **George** Allan **Webbe** (15 Jan 1854 London – 19 Feb 1925 Ascot, Berkshire) son of Alexander Webbe
  no issue
 6. **Hon. Francis Hay** (14 Aug 1864 Slains Castle – 24 Sep 1898 Queensland, Australia)
 7. **Lady Florence** Agnes Adelaide **Hay** (31 May 1872 Slains Castle – 16 Oct 1935)
  = 9 May 1895 Chelsea; **Henry Wolrige-Gordon** (1 Jan 1863 London – 9 Oct 1923) son of Henry Wolridge & Anne Gordon
  no issue
C. **Lady Agnes** Georgiana Elizabeth **Hay** (12 May 1829 London – 18 Dec 1869 London)
= 16 Mar 1846 Paris; **Sir James Duff KT, 5th Earl of Fife** Viscount Macduff, Baron Braco, **1st Baron Skeene** (6 Jul 1814 Banffshire – 7 Aug 1879 Braemar, Aberdeenshire) son of Sir Alexander Duff & Anne Stein; suc.uncle as Earl 9 Mar 1857; cr. Baron Skeene 2 Mar 1860; KT 1860
 1. **Lady Anne** Elizabeth Clementina **Duff** (16 Aug 1847 Edinburgh- 31 Dec 1925)
  = 17 Oct 1865 Brighton; **Sir John** Villiers Stuart **Townshend, 5th Marquess Townshend** Viscount Raynham, Baron Townshend, **10th Baronet** (10 Apr 1831 Brighton – 26 Oct 1899) son of Sir John Townshend, 4th Marquess Townshend & Elizabeth Stuart; suc. father as Marquess 10 Sep 1863
  a. **Sir John** James Dudley Stuart **Townshend, 6th Marquess Townshend** etc.(17 Oct 1866 London – 17 Nov 1921) suc.father

as Marquess 26 Oct 1899
= 9 Aug 1905; **Gwladys** Ethel Gwendolen Eugenie **Sutherst** (1885 – 10 Oct 1959) daughter of Thomas Sutherst; =2nd Bernard le Strange

I) **Sir George** John Patrick Dominic **Townshend, 7th Marquess Townshend** etc.(13 May 1916 – 27 Apr 2010) suc. father as Marquess 17 Nov 1921
=1 2 Sep 1939 (dv.1960); **Elizabeth** Pamela Audrey **Luby** (29 Sep 1915 - 1989) daughter of Thomas Luby; =2nd Sir James Gault
=2 22 Dec 1960; **Ann** Frances **Darlow** (29 Jan 1932 - 1988) daughter of Arthur Darlow
=3 7 May 2004 Fakenham, Norfolk; **Philippa** Sophia **Montgomerie** (*25 Apr 1935) daughter of George Kidston-Montgomerie of Southanan & Lydia Mason; =1st Humphrey Swire
issue of 1st:

A) **Lady Carolyn** Elizabeth Ann **Townshend** (*27 Sep 1940) resumed her maiden name
=1 13 Oct 1962 (dv.1968); **Antonio Capellini** (…) son of Vincenzo Capellini & Donna Anna Candeo Vanzetti Levida Zara
=2 Jan 1973 (ann.1974); **Edgar** Miles **Bronfman** (*20 Jun 1929) son of Samuel Bronfman & Saidye …; =1st Ann Loeb, he =3rd (married twice) Georgiana Webb, =4th Jan Aronson;
issue of 1st (none by 2nd):

1) **Vincenzo** Charles **Capellini Townshend** (*1963)
   = 1994; **Rachel Daniels** (…) daughter of Mark Daniels
   a) **Luca** Charles **Capellini Townshend** (*Feb 1995 Ipswich)
   b) **Sofia** Elizabeth **Capellini Townshend** (*Jul 1996 Ipswich)
   c) **Luisa** Carolyn **Capellini Townsherd** (* Sep 1998 Ipswich)

B) **Lady Joanna** Agnes **Townshend** (*19 Aug 1943) resumed her maiden name
=1 27 Sep 1962 (dv.1968); **Jeremy** George Courtnay **Bradford** (…) son of George Bradford
=2 1 Jan 1978 (dv.1984); **James** Barry **Morrissey** (*… Boston)
=3 1991; **Christian** Marc **Boegner** (…) son of Etienne Boegner

issue of 1st (none of others):
1) **Francis** James Patrick **Bradford** (*28 Oct 1963)
C) **Charles** George **Townshend, 8th Marquess of Townshend** etc.(*26 Sep 1945)
=1 8 Oct 1975; **Hermoine Ponsonby** (23 Jan 1945 - 1985) killed in car crash; daughter of Robert Ponsonby & Dorothy Lane; =1st Anthony Evans
=2 1990; **Alison Combs** (...) daughter of Sir Willis Combs; she =1st ... Marshall
issue 1st (none by 2nd):
1) **Thomas** Charly, **Viscount Raynham** (*2 Nov 1977)
= 2010/2011; **Octavia** Christina **Legge** (*1980 London) daughter of Christopher Legge & Sarah Marshall
2) **Hon. Louise** Elizabeth **Townshend** (*23 Jul 1979)
= 2006; **Edson da Paixao**(...)
issue of 2nd:
D) **Lord John** Patrick **Townshend** (*17 Jun 1962)
=1 12 Sep 1988 Wadour Castle, Tisbury, Wiltshire (dv.1991); **Rachel** Lucy **Chapple** (*1960) daughter of Sir John Chapple
=2 23 Sep 1999 London; **Helen Chin-Choy** (*17 Jun 1960 Bracknell) daughter of Larry Chin-Choy & Cathy Oatham; =1st William Burt
issue of 2nd (none by 1st):
1) **Isobel** Ann **Townshend** (*27 Jul 2001 London)
2) **George** Ivan **Townshend** (*Nov 2003 London)
E) **Lady Katherine** Anne **Townshend** (*29 Sep 1963)
=1 Apr 1991 (dv.2000); **Piers W Dent** (*1963) son of Robin Dent & Diana Delap; =2nd Katherine Steel
=2 Aug 2001; **Guy** Langford **Bayley** (*1964)
issue of 1st
1) **Lucia Dent** (*1992)
2) **Mollie** Elsa **Dent** (*Oct 1995 Gloucester)
issue of 2nd:
3) **Inca** Nell **Bayley** (*15 Feb 2001 Bristol)
4) **Skye** Georgina **Bayley** (*24 Oct 2002)
II) **Lady Elizabeth** Mary Gladys **Townshend** (16 Oct 1917 – 31 Dec 1950)
=1 20 Oct 1939 (dv.1947); **Sir** Eric **Richard** Meadows **White, 2nd Baronet** (29 Jun 1910 – 26 Apr 1972) son of Sir Robert White, 1st Baronet & Rose Pearce-Senocold; =2nd

Ann Eccles
=2 15 Mar 1949; **John** Clifford **Roberts** (…) son of John Roberts
issue of 1st (none 2nd):
- A) **Sir Christopher** Robert Meadows **White, 3rd Baronet** (*26 Aug 1940) suc.father as Baronet 26 Apr 1972
  =1 14 Apr 1962 (dv.1967); **Anne** Marie Ghislaine **Brown** (…) daughter of Thomas Brown
  =2 1968 (dv.1972); **Dinah** Mary **Sutton** (…)
  =3 1976; **Ingrid** Carolyn **Jowett** (*1947) daughter of Eric Jowett & Madaline Jeary
  no issue

b. **Lady Agnes** Elizabeth Audrey **Townshend** (12 Dec 1870 London – 15 Mar 1955)
= 2 Sep 1903; **James** Andrew **Cunninghame-Durham** (8 Aug 1879 – 30 Sep 1954) son of James Durham & Anne Duke
- I) **Nicholas** James Redvers Johan Townshend **Cunninghame-Durham** (13 Jan 1905 London – 17 Mar 1943 Mareth) killed in action
  = 26 Mar 1934; **Joyce** Wynyard **DuPre** (9 Feb 1912 London – …) daughter of William DuPre & Youri Wight
  no issue
- II) **Victoria** Townshend **Cunninghame-Durham** (9 Apr 1908 London – 7 Dec 2002)

2. **Lady Ida** Louise Alice **Duff** (10 Dec 1848 Duff House – 29 May 1918)
=1 3 Jun 1867 Garendon Park, Leicestershire (dv.1873); **Adrian** Elias **Hope** (8 Apr 1845 – 18 Nov 1914) son of John Hope & Countess Mathilde Rapp; =2nd Mildred Scott
=2 20 Sep 1880 London (dv.); **William Wilson** (1844 – 16 Feb 1905 Derby)
issue of 1st (none by 2nd):
a. **Agnes** Henrietta Ida May **Hope** (1868 London – 15 Jul 1920 London)
= 28 Aug 1889 Garendon Park; **Edwin** Joseph Lisel **March Phillipps de Lisle** (13 Jun 1852 – 5 May 1920) son of Ambrose de Lisle & Laura Clifford
- I) **Mary** Agnes Adeodata **March Phillipps de Lisle** (13 Jun 1890 London - Oct 1944)
  = 22 Apr 1914; **Dino, Count Spetia di Radione** (14 Jan 1882 Fossombrone - 20 Nov 1958 San Remo) son of Alessandro,

Count Spetia di Radione & Antonietta Dona; =2ⁿᵈ Gladys McConnell
  A) **Paganello dei conti Spetia** (1 Apr 1917 Ferrara - 1995)
II) **John** Adrian Frederick **March Phillipps de Lisle** (27 Sep 1891 London – 4 Nov 1961)
  = 12 Jul 1924; **Elizabeth** Muriel Sarah Smythe **Guinness** (20 Jan 1892 – 30 Mar 1974) daughter of Robert Guinness & Lydia Smythe
  A) **Alathea** Henriette Mary **March Phillipps de Lisle** (14 May 1925 – 11 Nov 2008 Lamastre Ardech, France)
    = 25 Jul 1953; **George** Hamilton **Boyle** (15 Sep 1928 – 27 Apr 2007) son of Edmund Boyle & Maida Evans-Freke
    1) **Robert** Edmund John **Boyle** (*28 Sep 1954)
      = 1985; **Gabrielle** Georgiana **Smollet** (*7 Jul 1960) daughter of Patrick Smollet
      a) **Albinia** Mary **Boyle** (*1988)
      b) **Patrick** Gordon Tobias **Boyle** (*1991)
    2) **Richard** William **Boyle** (*8 Jan 1959)
      = 1990; **Suzanne** Jean **Bingham** (*1963) daughter of Charles Bingham
      a) **Clementine** Pamela **Boyle** (*1997)
      b) **Jonathan** Charles **Boyle** (*2001)
    3) **Rupert** Lancelot Cavendish **Boyle** (*19 Sep 1960)
      = 1986; **Sarah** Daphne **Berry** (*1963) daughter of Simon Berry
      a) **Angus** Hugo Edmund **Boyle** (*1989)
      b) **Christopher** Simon Hamilton **Boyle** (*1992)
      c) **Jocelyn** William Rupert **Boyle** (*6 Apr 1998)
  B) **Elizabeth** Catherine Denise **March Phillipps de Lisle** (*19 Aug 1927)
    = 24 Jan 1951; **Jeremy** Anthony **White** (*13 Jan 1926) son of Anthony White & Flora Scott
    1) **Philippa** Elizabeth **White** (*12 Jun 1952)
    2) **Juliet** Anne **White** (*15 Feb 1955)
      = 7 May 1983; **Peter** Anthony **Fenton** (*1955) son of Mark Fenton
      a) **Emily** Victoria **Fenton** (*26 Jan 1986)
      b) **Christopher** Belmont **Fenton** (*8 Jul 1888)
    3) **Anthony** John **White** (*8 Jan 1958)
      = 18 Oct 1982; **Tessa** Marion **Hugo** (*1960) daughter of Sir John Hugo

a) **Zara** Elizabeth Hugo **White** (*21 Dec 1987)
   b) **Charlotte** Antonia **White** (*24 May 1989)
   c) **Serena** Isabel **White** (*16 Jun 1992)
  4) **Annabel** Mary **White** (*1 Jan 1962)
   = 28 Aug 1990; Hugh **Edward** John **Montgomery** (*1960) son of Hugh Montgomery
   a) **Alexander** Charles **Montgomery** (*4 Jul 1993)
   b) **James** Anthony **Montgomery** (*29 Oct 1995)
   c) **Nicholas** Rollo **Montgomery** (*8 Oct 1999)
C) **Everard** John Robert **March Phillipps de Lisle** (8 Jun 1930 Snitterfield, Warwickshire– 30 Apr 2003 Stanion, Northampton) killed in a car crash
 = 2 Apr 1959 London; **Hon. Mary** Rose **Peake** (*23 Apr 1940 Welwyn, Hertfordshire) daughter of Osbert Peake, 1st Viscount Ingleby & Lady Joan Capell
 1) **Charles** Andrew Everard **March Phillipps de Lisle** (*18 Aug 1960 London)
  = Sept 2003 Leicester; **Sharon** Rachel **Davis** (*1969) daughter of Eric Davis; =1st ... Abelman
  a) **Charlotte** India Rose **March Phillipps de Lisle** (*26 Nov 2006)
 2) **Timothy** John **March Phillipps de Lisle** (*25 Jun 1962 London)
  = 4 May 1991 Compton, Berkshire; **Amanda** Helen **Barford** (*1964 London) daughter of Clive Barford & Helen Foster
  a) **Daniel** Barford **March Phillipps de Lisle** (*24 Jan 1994 London)
  b) **Laura** Jane **March Phillipps de Lisle** (*20 Apr 1998 London)
 3) Mary **Rosanna March Phillipps de Lisle** (*18 May 1968 London)
  has issue:
  a) **Arthur** Rowan Luke **de Lisle** (*26 Aug 2010 London)
D) **Julian** Peter Alexander **March Phillipps de Lisle** (2 Feb 1936 Snitterfield, Warwickshire - 19 Dec 1993 Medbourne, Leicestershire)
 =1 1968 London (dv.1970); **Judith A Howard** (...)
 =2 21 Apr 1971 London; **Diana** Barbara **Welchman** (*14 Mar 1944 Minehead, Somerset) daughter of John Welchman & Valerie Riley
 issue of 2nd:

1) **Alexandra** Elizabeth Hope **March Phillipps de Lisle** (*12 Jul 1972 London)
= 24 Oct 2009 Medbourne; **Shamus** Diarmid **Ogilvy** (*24 Jan 1966 London) son of Hon. James Ogilvy & June Ducas
   a) **Angus** Julian Frederick **Ogilvy** (*21 Aug 2010)
2) **Clare** Catherine Alice **March Philipps de Lisle** (*29 Jan 1975 London)
3) **John** Julian Edward **March Phillipps de Lisle** (*14 Aug 1977 London)
= 11 Jul 2009 Anglesey, Wales; **Flor Gruffudd Jones** (...) daughter of Dafydd Grufford Jones
   a) **Zinnia** Alice Victoria **March Phillipps de Lisle** (*8 Jan 2011)
III) **Rudolph** Henry Edward **March Phillipps de Lisle** (11 Nov 1892 – 17 Aug 1943)
IV) **Sister Bertha** Mary Henriette **March Phillipps de Lisle** (6 Nov 1893 Garendon Park - 1973 London)
V) **Ambrose** Paul Jordan **March Phillipps de Lisle** (15 Nov 1894 Garendon Park – 8 Sep 1963)
= 2 Dec 1939; **Christiane de Conchy** (1908 - 10 May 2001) daughter of ..., Baron de Conchy
A) **Gerard March Phillipps de Lisle** (*20 Sep 1940)
= 1965; **Edith Karup** (*1938)
  1) **Frederick March Phillipps de Lisle** (*1957)
  = 1986; **Hon. Aubyn** Cecilia **Hovell-Thurlow-Cumming-Bruce**[21] (*1958) daugher of Francis Hovell-Thurlow-Cumming-Bruce, 8th Baron Thurlow & Yvonne Wilson
    a) **James** Gerard **March Phillipps de Lisle** (*1987)
    b) **Ralph** Francis **March Phillipps de Lisle** (*1989)
    c) **Rosalie** Yvonne **March Phillipps de Lisle** (*1991)
  2) **Peter** Andrew Paul **March Phillipps de Lisle** (*1959)
  = 1984; **Leanda Dormer** (*1959)
    a) **Rupert** Gerard Xavier **March Phillipps de Lisle** (*1986 London)
    b) **Christian** Michael Frederick **March Phillipps de Lisle** (*1988 London)
    c) **Dominic** Robert Peter **March Phillipps de Lisle** (*1990 London)

---

[21] Aubyn is the sister of Miranda who married Michael Gurney

B) Ambrose Bertram (**Bertie**) **March Phillipps de Lisle** (*8 Jul 1945)
= 1972; **Catherine Renardier** (*1947)
1) **Alexia March Phillipps de Lisle** (*1973)
2) **Edward** Ambrose **March Phillipps de Lisle** (*1976 London)
= 2006; **Sarah Rawstron** (*1977)
a) **Zac March Phillipps de Lisle** (*2008)
b) a child (*2009)
3) **Jasmine** Mary **March Phillipps de Lisle** (*1982 London)
= 2009; **Michael Jardine** (*1981)
no issue
C) **Hubert March Phillipps de Lisle** (*15 Aug 1946)
= 1976 Paris; **Marie-Dominique Quentin** (*1946)
1) **Geraldine** Marie **March Phillipps de Lisle** (*1978)
= 15 Sep 2007 La Roche-Posay, France; **John** Patrick **Arbuthnott** (*1977) son of James Arbuthnott & Hon. Louisa Hughes-Young
a) due Jul 2011
2) **Thomas March Phillipps de Lisle** (*24 Oct 1979 in Germany)
= 14 Jun 2008 Hindon, Wilts; **Caroline Budge** (*7 Mar 1981 London) daughter of David Budge & Sarah McClintock
a) **Maximilian** Lancelot Hubert **March Phillipps de Lisle** (*8 Nov 2009 London)
D) **Edwin** Rudolph Joseph **March Phillipps de Lisle** (*2 Feb 1948)
= 1979 Tur Langton; **Caroline** Astrid **Rowley** (*28 Jun 1955) daughter of Sir Charles Rowley, 8th Baronet & Astrid Massey
1) **Alexander** Edwin **March Phillipps de Lisle** (*9 Dec 1983 Kettering)
= 9 Oct 2010 Long Clawson; **Hannah Day** (*8 May 1980 Nottingham) daughter of Charles Day & Pamela ...
a) **Hugo** Charles **March Phillipps de Lisle** (*16 Jun 2009 Singapore)
2) **Nicholas** Charles **March Phillipps de Lisle** (*24 May 1991 London)
VI) **Lancelot** Joseph Everard **March Phillipps de Lisle** (22 Nov 1895 Garendon Park – 25 Sep 1928)
VII) **Alexander** Charles Nicholas **March Phillipps de Lisle** (6

171

Dec 1896 Garendon Park – 20 Nov 1917) killed in action
  VIII) **Sister Philomena** Edwina Dolores **March Phillipps de Lisle** (13 Feb 1903 Garendon Park – 1969 London)
  b. **Mildred** Louisa Annie **Hope** (15 Jun 1869 London - 1957) = 24 Jun 1909 London; **Robert** Astley **Smith** (1865 Brampton Ash, Northamptonshire - 1913) son of Rev. Sydney Smith & Hon. Frances Scarlett
  no issue
  c. **Ethel** Alexina Agnes **Hope** (1871 London - 1967 London) = 21 Apr 1903 London (dv.); **John** Percy **Lockhart Mummery** (14 Feb 1875 Northolt – 24 Apr 1957 Hove); =2nd Georgette Maier
  no issue
3. **Sir Alexander** William George **Duff, KG, KT, GCVO, 1st Duke of Fife** Marquess of Macduff, Earl of Macduff, **6th Earl of Fife** etc, **2nd Baron Skeene**[22] (10 Nov 1849 Edinburgh – 29 Jan 1912 Aswan, Egypt) suc.father as Earl of Fife, etc.7 Aug 1879; cr. Duke of Fife and Marquess of Macduff 29 Jul1889; cr. Earl of Macduff 16 Oct 1889[23]; KT1881, GCVO 1901, KG 1911
  = 27 Jul 1889 Buckingham Palace; **HRH Princess Louise** Victoria Alexandra Dagmar **of Great Britain and Ireland, The Princess Royal** Princess of Saxe-Coburg and Gotha, Duchess of Saxony (20 Feb 1867 London – 4 Jan 1931 London) daughter of Edward VII, King of the United Kingdom & Princess Alexandra of Denmark; usage of the Saxon titles was discontinued 17 Jul 1917
  a. a son (stillborn 16 Jun 1890 Richmond)
  b. **HH Princess Alexandra** Victoria Alberta Edwina Louise **of Fife, (2nd) Duchess of Fife** Countess of Macduff (17 May 1891 Richmond – 26 Feb 1959 London) nee Lady Alexandra Duff, cr. Princess 9 Nov 1905 by grandfather; suc.father as Duchess 29 Jan 1912
  = 15 Oct 1913 London; **Prince Arthur** Frederick Patrick Albert **of Connaught, Prince of Geat Britain and Ireland** (and Prince of Saxe-Coburg and Gotha, Duke of Saxony until 17 Jul 1917) (13 Jan 1883 Windsor – 12 Nov 1938 London) son of Prince Arthur, 1st Duke of Connaught and Stathearn & Princess Luise Margarete of Prussia

---

[22] Upon the death of the 1st Duke of Fife, all of his titles except the Dukedom of Fife and the Earldom of Macduff became extinct.
[23] The Dukedom of Fife and Earldom of Macduff were recreated in 1900 to include the daughters of the 1st Duke.

I) **Alastair** Arthur **Windsor**[24], **2ⁿᵈ Duke of Connaught and Stratherarn,** Earl of Sussex (9 Jul 1914 London – 26 April 1943 Ottawa, Canada) suc.grandfather as Duke 12 Sep 1938 and was heir-apparent to the Dukedom of Fife at the time of his death
 c. **HH Princess Maud** Alexandra Georgina Bertha **of Fife** (3 Apr 1893 Richmond – 14 Dec 1945 London) née Lady Maud Duff, cr. Princess 9 Nov 1905 by grandfather
  = 12 Nov 1923 London; **Charles** Alexander **Carnegie,**[25] **11ᵗʰ Earl of Southesk**, Lord Carnegie, Baron Balinhard (23 Sep 1893 Edinburgh – 16 Feb 1992 Kinnaird Castle) son of Charles Carnegie, 10ᵗʰ Earl of Southesk & Ethel Bannerman
   I) **James** George Alexander Bannerman **Carnegie, 3ʳᵈ Duke of Fife**, Earl of Macduff, **12ᵗʰ Earl of Southesk** etc.(*23 Sep 1929 London) suc.aunt as Duke 26 Feb 1959; suc.father as Earl of Southesk 14 Feb 1992
    = 11 Sep 1954 Perth (dv.1966); **Hon. Caroline** Cecily **Dewar** (*12 Feb 1934 Milngavie) daughter of Alexander Dewar, 3ʳᵈ Baron Forteviot & Cynthia Starkie
    A) a son (stillborn 4 Apr 1958)
    B) **Lady Alexandra** Clare **Carnegie** (*20 Jun 1959)
     = 11 May 2001 London; **Mark** Fleming **Etherington** (*10 Dec 1952 Newmarket, Ontario) son of Donald Etherington & Mary Mercer
     1) **Amelia** Mary Carnegie **Etherington** (*24 Dec 2001 London)
    C) **David** Charles, **Earl of Southesk** (*3 Mar 1961 London)
     = 16 Jul 1987 London; **Caroline** Anne **Bunting** (*13 Nov 1961 Windsor) daughter of Martin Bunting & Veronica Cope
     1) **Charles** Duff, **Lord Carnegie** (*1 Jul 1989 Edinburgh)
     2) **Hon. Georg** William **Carnegie** (*23 Mar 1991 Edinburgh)
     3) **Hon. Hugh** Alexander **Carnegie** (*6 Oct 1993 Dundee)
 4. **Lady Agnes** Cecil Emmeline **Duff** (18 May 1852 London – 11 Jan 1925 Cimiez, France)
  =1 4 Oct 1871 (dv.1876); **George** Robert, **Viscount Dupplin** (27 May 1849 London – 10 Mar 1886 Perthshire) son of George Hay-

---

[24] Titled Prince of Great Britain, Prince of Saxe-Coburg and Gotha, Duke of Saxony until 1917 when Royal Decrees were issued discontinuing the use of the German titles and then restricting the royal titles to children and grandchildren of a Sovereign. Alistair was a great-grandson of Queen Victoria and there for was not longer styled Prince.
[25] The 11ᵗʰ Earl of Southesk was the uncle of Raymond Carnegie who married Diana, Countess of Erroll

Drummond, 12th Earl of Kinnoull & Lady Emily Somerset; heir-apparent to father at time of his death
=2 5 Aug 1876 London; **Herbert Flower** (1851 Bath – 30 Dec 1880 London) son of Philip Flower & Mary Flower
=3 4 Jul 1882 London; **Sir Alfred Cooper, Kt.** (1838 Norwich – 3 Mar 1908) son of William Cooper & Anna Marsh; Kt. 1902
issue of 1st:
a. **Hon. Agnes** Blanche Marie **Hay-Drummond** (6 Dec 1873 London – 13 Dec 1938)
   = 21 Feb 1903 Rome; **Herbert von Beneckendorff und Hindenburg** (1 Apr 1872 Berlin – 31 Jul 1956 Burg Bassenheim, Germany) son of Konrad von Beneckendorff und Hindenburg & Countess Sophie zu Münster
   I) **Marie von Beneckendorff und Hindenburg** (* & + 25 Dec 1903)
issue of 3rd (none by 2nd):
b. **Stephanie** Agnes **Cooper** (5 Sep 1883 London – 9 Dec 1918)
   =1 19 Dec 1903 London; **Arthur** Francis **Levita** (15 Feb 1865 Manchester - 18 Nov 1910) son of Emile Levita & Catherine Rée
   =2 10 Oct 1916; **Maurice** ffolliot Rhys **Wingfield** (8 Sep 1879 Stow on Wold, Gloucestershire – 9 Apr 1941) son of Edward Wingfield & Edith Wood; =1st Lydia Rudge; = 3rd Muriel Dunsmuir
   issue of 1st (none by 2nd):
   I) **Violet** Frances **Levita** (10 Sep 1904 London – 1999 London)
      =1 9 Nov 1926 London (dv.1933); **Richard** Barrow **Hirsch** (1899 London – 11 May 1947) son of Leopold Hirsch & Mathilde ...
      =2 24 Dec 1937 Mumbai, India (dv.); **Ronald Critchley** (Aug 1905 - ...) son of Edward Critchley & Elizabeth Critchley; =2nd Contance Byass
      issue of 1st (none by 2nd):
      A) **Nicholas** F **Hirsch** (1930 London – 3 Oct 1983 Dunning Perthshire)
         = 3 Jun 1965; **Barbara Peacocke** (... – 22 May 1976) killed in a car crash
         no issue
   II) **Enid** Agnes Maud **Levita** (10 Feb 1908 London - 1993)
      =1 17 Dec 1930 (dv.); **Euan** Donald **Cameron** (1906 -

1958) son of Ewen Cameron & Rachel Granger; =2nd
Marielen von Meiss-Teuffem
=2 1961; **Hon. Robert** Fraser **Watson** (1901 - 1975) son of
Joseph Watson, 1st Baron Manton & Claire Nickols
issue of 1st (none by 2nd):
A) **Ian** Donald **Cameron** (1 Oct 1932 Blairmore House, Huntly, Aberdeen – 8 Sep 2010 Toulon)
= 20 Oct 1962; **Mary** Fleur **Mount** (*22 Oct 1934) daughter of Sir William Mount, 2nd Baronet & Elizabeth Llewellyn
  1) **Allan** Alexander **Cameron** (*27 Aug 1963 London)
  = 19 May 1990 London; **Sarah** Louise **Fearnley-Whittingstall** (*23 Jul 1963) daughter of William Fearnley-Whittingstall & Daphne Shortt
    a) **Imogen** Clare **Cameron** (*3 Oct 1992 London)
    b) **Angus Cameron** (*8 Oct 1994 London)
  2) **Tania** Rachel **Cameron** (*7 Mar 1965 London)
  = 9 Sep 1995 Peasemore, Berkshire; **Carl** I O **Brookes** (…)
    a) **Oliver** Aiden **Brookes** (* May 2002 London)
  3) **Rt.Hon. David** William Donald **Cameron** (*9 Oct 1966 London) Prime Minister since 2010
  = 1 Jun 1996 East Hendred, Oxfordshire; **Samantha** Gwendolen **Sheffield** (*1971 London) daughter of Sir Reginald Sheffield, 8th Baronet & Annabel Jones[26]
    a) **Ivan** Reginald Ian **Cameron** (8 Apr 2002 London – 25 Feb 2009 London)
    b) **Nancy** Gwendoline **Cameron** (*19 Jan 2004 London)
    c) **Arthur** Elwen **Cameron** (*14 Feb 2006 London)
    d) **Florence** Rose Endelion **Cameron** (*24.10.2010 Truro, Cornwall)
  4) **Clare** Louise **Cameron** (*1971 London)
  = 24 Apr 2010 Peasemore; **Jeremy Fawcus** (...) son of Graham Fawcus & Diana Spencer-Philips
    a) **Molly Fawcus** (*23 Dec 2010)
c. **Hermione** Mary Louise **Cooper** (11 May 1885 London - Nov 1923 Wiesbaden, Germany)
= 1904 London; **Neil Duff Arnott** (1870 London - 16 Jun

---

[26] Annabel Jones later married the 4th Viscount Astor, half brother of Hon. Emily Astor (another William IV descendant).

1929 London) son of ...; =1ˢᵗ Evelyn Hewlett
I) **Ian** Neil **Duff Arnott** (1905 London - 1950 London)
= 1930 London; **Phyllis** Mary S **Innes** (1908 Plymouth, Devonshire - 1956 Birmingham)
  A) **Portia Duff Arnott** (1 Jan 1931 London - 2009 Cyprus)
    = ..; **James Lord** (...)
    1) **Simon** M D **Lord** (*1959 Portsmouth)
      = Dec 1986; **Sarah** A **Pyne** (*1959)
      a) **Victoria** Catherine **Lord** (*Feb 1988 London)
      b) **Alice** Elizabeth **Lord** (*May 1991)
      c) **Olivia** Charlotte **Lord** (*Oct 1993)
    2) **Alexandra Lord** (*1962)
      = Jul 1997; **Miguel Buceta San Martin** (*...) son of Luis San martin
      a) a daughter (...)
      b) a son (...)
  B) **Tancred Duff Arnott** (* & + 1934 Birmingham)
d. **Sybil** Mary **Cooper** (26 Nov 1886 London – 3 Jan 1927 London)
= 19 Jan 1904 London; **Richard** Vaughan **Hart-Davis** (1 May 1878 Farnham, Surrey – 26 Aug 1964 London) son of Henry Hart-Davis & Anne Whittingham
  I) **Sir Rupert** Charles **Hart-Davis, Kt**[27] (28 Aug 1907 London – 8 Dec 1999 Northallerton, Yorkshire) knighted 1967
  =1 23 Dec 1929 London (dv.1933); Edith Margaret (**Peggy**) **Ashcroft** (later Dame Peggy, DBE) (22 Oct 1907 Croydon – 14 Jun 1991 London) daughter of William Ashcroft; DBE 1956; =2ⁿᵈ Theodore Komisarjevsky; =3ʳᵈ Jeremy Hutchinson, Baron Hutchinson of Lullington
  =2 25 Nov 1933 London (dv.1964); Catherine **Comfort Borden-Turner** (15 Aug 1910 – Aug 1970) daughter of George Turner & Mary Borden
  =3 19 Oct 1964 London; Winifred **Ruth Ware** (... - 31 Jan 1967 Edinburgh) =1ˢᵗ Oliver Simon
  =4 13 Jun 1968 Richmond; **June Clifford** (*1924) daughter of Arthur Clifford & Edith Bowell; =1ˢᵗ David Williams
  issue of 2ⁿᵈ (none by others):

---

[27] Although Richard Hart-Davis was Rupert's legal father, Rupert himself always intimated that his biological father was one Gervase Beckett.

A) **Bridget** Min **Hart-Davis** (*13 Jan 1935 London)
   = 1963 London; **Sir David** Malcolm **Trustram Eve, 2**nd **Baron Silsoe**, 2nd Baronet (2 May 1930– 31 Dec 2005 Reading) son of Sir Malcolm Trustram Eve, 1st Baron Silsoe & Marguerite Nanton; suc.father as Baron Dec 1976
   1) **Hon. Amy** Comfort **Trustram Eve** (*13 Jun 1964 London)
   2) **Sir Simon** Rupert **Trustram Eve, 3**rd **Baron Silsoe** etc.(*17 Apr 1966 London) suc.father as Baron 31 Dec 2005
B) Peter **Duff Hart-Davis** (*3 Jun 1936 London)
   = 22 Apr 1961 Builth Wells, Powys, Wales; Diana **Phyllida Barstow** (*30 Sep 1937 London) daughter of John Barstow & Diana Yarnton; =1st ... Mills
   1) **Alice Hart-Davis** (*27 May 1963 Builth Wells)
      = 19 Aug 1989; **Matthew** William **Hindhaugh** (*23 Aug 1958 Saltburn, Yorkshire) son of William Hindlaugh & Jenneth ...
      b) **Felicity** Mary **Hindhaugh** (*24 Feb 1995 London)
      c) **Elizabeth** Rose **Hindhaugh** (*9 Dec 1996 London)
      d) Robert **John Hindhaugh** (*4 Aug 1999 London)
   2) **Guy** Edward Peter **Hart-Davis** (*28 Nov 1964 Henley-on-Thames, Oxfordshire)
      =1 1991 Las Vegas; **Michele** C **Batcabe** (19 May 1965 - 8 Jan 1998)
      =2 2000; **Rhonda Holmes** (...)
      issue of 2nd (none by 1st):
      a) **Edward Hart-Davis** (*5 Sep 2000)
C) **Adam** John **Hart-Davis** (*4 Jul 1943 Henley-on-Thames)
   =1 21 Dec 1965 Oxford (dv.1995); **Adrienne Alpin** (17 Aug 1944 West Yorkshire - Jan 2005 Oxford) daughter of Joseph Alpin & Dorrien Heys
   =2 19 Jun 2010; **Susan Blackmore** (*29 Jul 1951)
   issue of 1st (none by 2nd):
   1) **Damon Hart-Davis** (*18 Aug 1967 Fulford, York)
      = ...; **Jean Ryder** (...)
      a) **Eloise Hart-Davis** (*14 Dec 2005)
   2) **Jason Hart-Davis** (*27 Aug 1971 Oxford)
      = 1996; **Michele Gunn** (...)
      a) **Louis** Sewavi Rupert **Hart-Davis** (*30 Dec 1997)

II) **Dierdre** Phyllis Ulrica **Hart-Davis** (5 Jul 1909 – 23 Nov 1998)
=1 24 Apr 1930 London; **Ronald** Egerton **Balfour** (1896 – 17 Apr 1941) killed in a car crash
=2 1946 London (dv.); **David Wolfers** (*1911 London) son of Samuel Wolfers & Sarah Delmonte
=3 35 Jul 1950 London; **Anthony** John **Bland** (1904 - Jan 1993) son of Jack Bland
=4 1978; **William Inman** (…)
issue of 1st:
A) **Susan** Mary **Balfour** (*30 Mar 1931 London)
B) **Annabel** Clare **Balfour** (*20 Oct 1935 London)
 = 15 Apr 1961 London; **Charles** Benedict **Rathbone** (...)
 1) **Paul** B **Rathbone** (*1962)
 2) **Oliver** A **Rathbone** (*1965)
   = May 1997 London; **Rachel Andrew** (...)
   a) **Alice** Eleanor **Rathbone** (*Jun 1998 London)
   b) **Marcus** Benedict **Rathbone** (*Sep 2000 London)
 3) **Benjamin** Charles **Rathbone** (*1967) (twin)
   = Jun 2001; **Lynn** Elaine **Huggins** (*1967 London) daughter of Michael Huggins & Peggy Balch
   a) **Willow** Eve **Rathbone** (*Nov 2004 Brighton)
 4) **Polly** Leonore **Rathbone** (*1967) (twin)
issue of 3rd (none by others):
C) Henrietta **Lucy Bland** (*1952 London)

e. **Sir** Alfred **Duff Cooper GCMG, 1st Viscount Norwich** (22 Feb 1890 London – 1 Jan 1954 at sea off coast of Vigo, Spain) cr. Viscount 5 Jul 1952
= 2 Jun 1919 London; **Lady Diana** Olivia Winifred Mard **Manners**[28] (29 Aug 1892 Uckfield, Sussex – 16 Jun 1986 London) daughter of Henry Manners, 8th Duke of Rutland & Violet Lindsay

I) **John Julius Cooper, 2nd Viscount Norwich** (*15 Sep 1929 London) suc.father as Viscount 1 Jan 1954
=1 5 Aug 1952 Guildford, Surrey (dv.1985); **Anne** Frances May **Clifford** (*5 Jan 1929) daughter of Hon. Sir Bede Clifford & Alice Gundry
=2 14 Jun 1989 London; **Hon. Mary Makins** (*11 Jul 1935)

---

[28] Lady Diana chose not to be known as Viscountess Norwich and retained the style Lady Diana Cooper after her husband's elevation to the peerage.

daughter of Roger Makins, 1st Baron Sherfield & Alice Davis;
she =1st Hon. Hugo Philipps (later 3rd Baron Milford)
issue of 1st (none by 2nd):
  A) **Hon.** Alice Clare Antonia Opportune (**Artemis**) **Cooper** (*22
     Apr 1953 London[29]) she has retained her maiden name
     = 1 Feb 1986; **Anthony** James **Beevor** (*1946 London) son of
     John Beevor
     1) **Eleanor** Allegra **Beevor** (*19 Jan 1990 London)
     2) **Adam** John Cosmo **Beevor** (*10 Feb 1993 London)
  B) **Hon. Jason** Charles Duff Bede **Cooper** (*29 Oct 1959
     Beirut, Lebanon) heir-apparent to Viscountcy
issue by **Enrica Soma** (May 1929 - Jan 1969) killed in a car
crash; wife of John Huston:
  C) **Allegra Huston** (*26 Aug 1964 London)
     issue by Francisco (**Cisco**) Antonio Miguel Niño de Ortíz
     Ladrón **de Guevara** (*24 Apr 1952 Las Alamos, New
     Mexico) son of Francisco Guevara & Emilia Luz Garcia
     Nuñez:
     1) **Rafael** Patrick Geronimo Niño de Ortíz Ladrón
        de Guervara (*30 Sep 2001 Taos, New Mexico)
issue by **Susan** Mary **Jay** (19 Jun 1918 Rome - 18 Aug 2004
Washington DC) daughter of Peter Jay & Susan Alexander;
wife of William Patten, Sr.; =2nd Joseph Alsop:
II) **William** Samuel **Patten Jr.** (*4 Jul 1948 Paris)
    =1 Sep 1970 Cambridge, Massachusetts; **Katharine Bacon**
    (...) daughter of Robert Bacon & Katharine Jay[30]
    =2 24 Nov 1999 Lancester, Massachusetts; **Sydney Camp**
    (*... Worcester, Massachusetts) daughter of ...; =1st ...
    Hayes
    issue of 1st:
    A) William **Samuel Patten** III (*1971 Washington, DC)
       = 1998; ...
       1) **Max Patten** (*29 Mar 1999 Camden)
    B) **Elizabeth** Anne **Patten** (*11 Apr 1974 Charlestown,
       Massachusetts)

---

[29] Artemis Cooper was born at the stroke of midnight between the 22nd and 23rd. Her parents opted to register the birth as the 22nd to avoid their daughter having to share her brithday with the Queen.

[30] William and Kate are 2nd cousins, their grandfathers, Peter and Delancy Jay, were brothers.

     = Aug 2002 Brooklyn, Maine; **Obediah Ostergard** (...)
     1) **Sophie** Morgan **Patten-Ostergard** (*2004)
     2) **Cyrus Patten-Ostergard** (...)
    C) **Sybil** Alexandra **Patten** (*26 Oct 1978 Camden, Maine)
  5. **Lady Alexina Duff** (1851 – 30 Apr 1882 London)
    = 22 Jul 1870 Severn Stoke, Worcestershire; **Henry** Aubrey **Coventry** (10 Oct 1846 Windsor – 13 May 1909) son of Hon. Henry Coventry & Caroline Dundas; =2nd Mary Miles
    no issue
 D. **Lady Alice** Mary Emily **Hay** (7 Jul 1835 – 7 Jun 1881)
    = 16 May 1874; **Charles** Edward Louis Philip Casimir **Stuart**[31] (1824 – 24 Dec 1880) son of Charles Allen & Anna Beresford
    no issue
VII. **Lord Adolphus FitzClarence** (18 Feb 1802 Bushy Park – 17 May 1856 Easingwold, Yorkshire)
VIII. **Lady Augusta FitzClarence** (17 Nov 1803 Bushy Park – 8 Dec 1865)
=1 5 Jul 1827 Bushy Park; **Hon. John Kennedy-Erskine** (4 Jun 1802 Dun House, Montrose – 6 Mar 1831) son of Archibald Kennedy, 1st Marquess of Ailsa & Margaret Erskine
=2 24 Aug 1836 Windsor Castle; **Lord John** Frederick **Gordon** (15 Aug 1799 – 29 Sep 1878 Kettins, Forfarshire) son of George Gordon, 9th Marquess of Huntley & Catherine Cope
issue of 1st (none by 2nd):
A. **William** Henry **Kennedy-Erskine** (1 Jul 1828 Dun House – 15 Dec 1870)
   = 18 Nov 1862; **Catherine Jones** (1840 – 13 Feb 1914) daughter of William Jones
   1. **Violet** Augusta Mary Frederica **Kennedy-Erskine** (1 Sep 1863 – 9 Sep 1946)
      = 27 Oct 1894; **Arthur** Otway **Jacob** (28 Aug 1867 Laoighis, Ireland - 1936) son of David Jacob & Sarah Fishbourne
      a. **Arthur** Henry Augustus **Jacob** (1895 – 16 Jul 1916 Calais, France) killed in action
   2. **Augustus** John William Henry **Kennedy-Erskine** (12 Apr 1866 – 2 Feb 1908)

---

[31] Both he and his father called themselves Count of Albany, based on a fantastical claim they were legitimately descended from King James II in the male line. Charles' birth was registered with the name Stuart but his father was legally names Allen. The senior Charles pretended to the name Stuart.

= 3 Nov 1896 London; **Alice** Marjorie Cunningham **Foote** (... - 3 Jul 1947)
   a. **Violet** Marjorie Augusta **Kennedy-Erskine** (1897 – 25 Dec 1934 London)
   b. **Millicent** Alison Augusta **Kennedy-Erskine** (1899 - 1980 Montrose, Aberdeen)
   = 17 Jul 1943; **Thomas** Maitland **Lovett** (29 May 1893 - 1946) son of Hubert Lovett & Lina Howard Brookes; =1st Millisainte ...; =2nd Morah Brunskill
   no issue
   c. **Augustus** John **Kennedy-Erskine** (14 Nov 1900 - +young) (twin)
   d. **William** Henry **Kennedy-Erskine** (14 Nov 1900 – 21 May 1963) (twin)
   = 1944; Beatrice **Doreen Plews** (1907 - May 1992 London); she =1st ... Croall; =2nd Gerard van de Linde
   no issue
  3. **Millicent** Augusta Vivian **Kennedy-Erskine** (12 Aug 1867 – 2 Nov 1883)
 B. **Wilhelmina Kennedy-Erskine** (27 Jun 1830 Dun – 9 Oct 1906 Brighton)
 = 1855; (her first cousin) **William FitzClarence, 2nd Earl of Munster** (1824 – 1901)
 see above
C. Augusta **Millicent** Anne Mary **Kennedy-Erksine** (11 May 1831 Windsor - 11 Feb 1895)
 = 17 May 1855 Wemyss Castle, Fife; **James** Hay **Erskine-Wemyss** (29 Aug 1829 Wemyss Castle – 29 Mar 1864) son of James Eskine-Wemyss & Lady Emma Hay[32]
  1. **Dora** Mina **Erskine-Wemyss** (6 Feb 1856 Wemyss Castle – 24 Dec 1894 Chester)
  = 21 Apr 1887 Wemyss Castle; **Lord Henry** George **Grosvenor** (23 Jun 1861 London – 27 Dec 1914) son of Sir Hugh Grosvenor, 1st Duke of Westminster & Lady Constance Leveson-Gower
   a. **Millicent** Constance **Grosvenor** (14 Jan 1889 – 24 Aug 1944)
   =1 15 Nov 1909 London (dv.1919); **William** Molyneux **Clarke** (28 Sep 1869 London - ...)
   =2 Aug 1919; **Frank Billinge** (1886 - 28 Dec 1928)

---

[32] Lady Emma was a sister of the 18th Earl of Erroll who married Lady Elizabeth FitzClarence

=3 6 Aug 1932; **John** Finlay **Dew** (1893 - ...) son of Rev. Edward Dew
issue by 1st (none by others)
  I) a son (* & + 1912)
b. **Lady Dorothy** Alice Margaret Augusta **Grosvenor** (22 Aug 1890 – 11 Jan 1966)
=1 15 Apr 1909 London (dv.1919); **Albert** Edward Harry Mayer Archibald, **Lord Dalmeny** (later **KT, 6**th **Earl of Rosebery**) (8 Jan 1882 – 30 May 1974) son of Archibald Primrose, 7th Earl of Rosebery & Hannah de Rothschild; suc.as Earl 21 May 1929; KT 1947; =2nd Hon. Eva Bruce
=2 16 Mar 1920 (dv.1927); **Robert** Bingham **Brassey** (18 Nov 1875 – 14 Nov 1946) son of Albert Brassey & Hon. Matilda Bingham; =1st Violet Lowry-Corry; =3rd Constance Britten
=3 26 May 1929 (dv.1938); **Chetwode** Charles Hamilton **Hilton-Green** (1895 - 31 Dec 1963) son of Francis Hilton-Green
=4 7 Feb 1938; **Richard** Herbert **Mack** (1886 in Norfolk - 6 Dec 1967) son of Philip Mack
issue of 1st (none by others):
  I) **Archibald** Ronald, **Lord Dalmeny** (1 Aug 1910 – 11 Nov 1931)
  II) **Lady Helen** Dorothy **Primrose** (1913 – 16 Oct 1998)
  = 26 Jun 1933; **Hon. Hugh** Adeane Vivian **Smith** (25 Apr 1910 – 20 Mar 1978) son of Vivian Smith, 1st Baron Bicester & Lady Sybil McDonnell
    A) **George** Harry Vivian **Smith** (*13 Jul 1934)
      =1 31 Jan 1962 (dv.1965); **June** Rose Jager **Foster-Towne** (...) daughter of Basil Foster-Towne & Diana Beatrice
      =2 16 Feb 1966; **Susan** Mary **Goodfellow** (...) daughter of Frank Goodfellow
      issue of 1st:
      1) **Charles** James **Smith** (*7 Sep 1963)
      issue of 2nd:
      2) **Sarah** Helen **Smith** (6 Nov 1968 – 27 Feb 1995)
      3) **Amanda** Mary **Smith** (*1 Sep 1972)
    B) **Elizabeth** Vivian **Smith** (*30 Mar 1939)
      = 26 Apr 1960; Alexander **James Macdonald-Buchanan** (*1931) son of Sir Reginald Macdonald Buchanan & Hon. Catherine Buchanan
      1) **Hugh** James **Macdonald-Buchanan** (*10 Sep 1961)
        = 2003; **Emma Wakefield** (...) daughter of John Wakefield

　　　　a) **Hector** Hugh John **Macdonald-Buchanan** (*2 Sep 2004)
　　　　b) **Matilda** Jessica Helen **Macdnald-Buchanan** (*18 May 2006)
　　2) **James** Iain Harry **Macdonald-Buchanan** (*4 Feb 1963)
　　　= 1996; **Julia Crossley** (*1960) daughter of Anthony Crossley & Jean Russell
　　　　a) **Angus** Anthony **Macdonald-Buchanan** (*1997)
　　　　b) **Flora** Ione **Macdonald-Buchanan** (*1999)
　　3) **Nicholas** Mark **Macdonald-Buchanan** (*26 Apr 1967)
　　　= 1996; **Vanessa Bates** (…) daughter of William Bates
　　　　a) **Archie** Nicholas **Macdonald-Buchanan** (*1998)
　　　　b) **Orlando Macdonald-Buchanan** (*2000)
　　4) Charles **Alexander Macdonald-Buchanan** (*1970)
　　　= 2011; **Poppy** Augusta **Fraser** (*1979) daughter of Hon. Hugh Fraser & Drusilla Montgomerie
　c. **William Grosvenor, 3rd Duke of Westminster**, etc.(23 Dec 1894 Chester – 22 Feb 1963) suc.cousin as Duke 19 Jul 1953
2. **Mary** Frances **Erskine-Wemyss** (30 Jun 1857 Edinburgh - 1923 Oakham, Rutland)
　= 28 Feb 1882 London; **Cecil** Stratford **Paget** (25 Sep 1856 London – 26 Feb 1936) son of Lord George Paget & Agnes Paget
　a. **Agnes** Millicent Augusta Dorothy Canning **Paget** (28 Mar 1883 London – 2 Jan 1935)
　b. **Henry** Forbridge **Paget** (17 Aug – 28 Nov 1886 London)
　c. **Louis** George **Paget** (26 Feb 1891 London - 13 Sep 1943 New Hampshire, USA)
　　= 29 Mar 1934 New York City; **Harriett Bullock** (…) daughter of George Bullock & …; =1st … Burton
　　no issue
3. **Randolph** Gordon **Erskine-Wemyss of Wemyss** (11 Jul 1858 – 17 Jul 1908)
　=1 18 Jul 1884 London (dv.1898); **Lady Lilian** Mary **Paulett** (26 Jul 1859 – 11 Nov 1952) daughter of John Paulett, 14th Marquess of Winchester & Hon. Mary Montagu
　=2 23 Nov 1898 London; **Lady Eva** Cecilia Margaret **Wellesley** (… - 4 Mar 1948) daughter of William Wellesley, 2nd Earl Cowley & Emily Williams
　issue of 1st (none by 2nd):
　a. **Mary** Millicent **Erskine-Wemyss** (15 May 1885 London - …)
　　= 30 Apr 1917; **Ernest** Casell **Long** (…)
　　no issue

b. **Michael** John **Wemyss of that Ilk** (8 Mar 1888 London - 1982) recognized as Head of the Wemyss Clan 1910
= 25 Nov 1918; **Lady Victoria** Alexandrina Violet **Cavendish-Bentinck** (27 Feb 1890 London – 8 May 1994 Wemyss Castle[33]) daughter of William Cavendish-Bentinck, 6th Duke of Portland & Winifred Dallas-Yorke
- I) **David Wemyss of that Ilk** (11 Feb 1920 – 26 Jan 2005 Invermay, Perth) suc. father as Head of the Wemyss Clan 1982
  = 21 Jul 1945; **Lady Jean** Christian **Bruce** (*12 Jan 1923) daughter of Edward Bruce, 14th Earl of Elgin and Kincardine & Hon. Katherine Cochrane
  - A) **Michael** James **Wemyss of that Ilk** (*10 Nov 1947) suc. father as Head of the Wemyss Clan 26 Jan 2005
    = 1975; **Charlotte** Mary **Bristowe** (…) daughter of Royle Bristowe
    - 1) **Hermione** Mary **Wemyss** (*1982)
      = 2006; **Thomas** Richard **Bell** (…) son of Peter Bell
    - 2) **Leonora** Anne **Wemyss** (*1986)
      = 14 Aug 2010; **Steven** L **Wendt** (...) son of Henry Wendt
  - B) **Charles** John **Wemyss** (*26 Jul 1952 Forteviot, Perth)
    = 21 Oct 1978 Sternfield, Suffolk; **Fiona** Elizabeth **Penn** (*12 Sep 1956 London) daughter of Sir Eric Penn & Prudence Stwart-Wilson
    - 1) **Mary** Victoria **Wemyss** (*20 Nov 1981 London)
    - 2) **Elizabeth** Katherine **Wemyss** (*8 Nov 1985 Edinburgh)
    - 3) **James** Michael **Wemyss** (*25 Jun 1987 Edinburgh)
  - II) **Andrew** Michael John **Wemyss** (*3 Oct 1925)
    = 8 Feb 1967; **Janet** Alethea **Scott** (19 May 1932 - 12 Feb 2006 London) daughter of John Scott & Althea Smith
    - A) **Isabella** Althea **Wemyss** (*22 Feb 1968)
    - B) **William** John **Wemyss** (*8 Oct 1970)
      = 3 May 2002; **Katherine Piper** (*6 Sep 1970) daughter of David Piper & Elizabeth Michell
      - 1) **Olivia Wemyss** (*6 Aug 2004) (twin)
      - 2) **Jonathan Wemyss** (*6 Aug 2004) (twin)
4. **Hugo Erskine-Wemyss** (31 May 1861 London – 12 Mar 1933)
5. **Sir Rosslyn** Erskine **Erskine-Wemyss GCB, 1st Baron Wester Wemyss** (12 Apr 1864 Wemyss Caslte – 24 May 1933

---

[33] Having lived to the age of 104, Lady Victoria Wemyss was the last living godchild of Queen Victoria.

Cannes) cr. Baron 18 Nov 1919[34]; GCB 1919
= 21 Dec 1903; **Victoria Morier** (… - 22 Apr 1945) daughter of Rt.Hon. Sir Robert Morier & Alice Peel
  a. **Hon. Alice** Elizabeth Millicent **Erskine-Wemyss** (1906 – 31 Dec 1994)
  = 11 Feb 1953; **Francis** Henry **Cunnack** (1899 in Cornwall – 5 Jan 1974)
  no issue

IX. **Rev. Lord Augustus FitzClarence** (1 Mar 1805 Bushy Park – 14 Jun 1854)
= 2 Jan 1845 London; **Sarah** Elizabeth Catherine **Gordon** (1827 – 23 Mar 1901 London) daughter of Lord Henry Gordon & Louisa Payne
 A. **Dorothea FitzClarence** (27 Oct 1845 London – 15 May 1870)
  = 17 Mar 1863; **Thomas** William **Goff** (6 Jul 1829 Oakport, co. Roscommon, Ireland – 3 Jun 1876) son of Thomas Goff & Anne Caulfield
  1. **Ethel** Anne **Goff** (12 Jan 1864 Roscommon, Ireland – 1 Mar 1928 London)
  =1 23 Dec 1885; **Henry** de Courcy **Agnew** (1 Nov 1851 – 6 Mar 1910) son of Sir Andrew Agnew, 8th Baronet & Lady Louisa Noel
  =2 27 Jul 1911 London; **Edmund Charrington** (1861 - May 1943) son of Thomas Charrington
  issue of 1st (none by 2nd):
   a. **Dorothea** Alma **Agnew** (1887 – 27 Feb 1969)
    = 14 May 1907 London; **Harold Swann** (29 Jan 1880 – 7 Nov 1953) son of Sir Charles Swann, 1st Baronet & Elizabeth Duncan
    I) **Helen Swann** (6 Oct – 8 Dec 1911)
    II) **Charles** Brian **Swann** (21 Jul 1913 – 7 Jan 1960)
    =1 9 Sep 1939 (dv.1955); **Vanessa** Fiaschi Dalrymple **Tennant** (23 Aug 1919 - 1995) daughter of Ernest Tennant & Leonora Fiaschi
    =2 8 Aug 1955; **Anne** Corben **Harrison** (…) daughter of Cyril Harrison; =1st John MacKinnon
    issue of 1st (none by 2nd):
    A) Julia **Vanessa Swann** (*30 Aug 1940)
     = 22 Oct 1960 (dv.); **Blyth** Metcalf **Thompson** (…)
     1) **Vanessa** Eirene **Thompson** (*17 Sep 1961)
     2) **William** Rowland **Thompson** (*14 Nov 1962)

---

[34] Lord Wester Wemyss' peerage became extinct upon his death.

      3) **Moya** Ann **Thompson** (*16 Oct 1965)
      4) **Hannah** Yvonne **Thompson** (*5 Jul 1967)
      5) **Sonya** Suzanne **Thompson** (*5 Jun 1969)
      6) **Denys** Martin Blythe **Thompson** (*1972)
    B) **Karin** Clarissa **Swann** (*8 Jun 1942)
    = 1977 London; **Michael** M **Grime** (*1941) son of Thomas Grime & Edith Pegler
    issue ?
    C) **Virginia** Caroline **Swann** (*31 Oct 1948)
    =1 28 Apr 1971 (dv.); **David** Winkfield **Hughes** (…)
    =2 …; **Edward** Willis **Fleming** (…)
    =3 …; **Michael Cann** (…)
    issue of 1st (none by others):
    1) **Harriet** Elfreda **Hughes** (*1972)
      = Sep 1998 London; **Blake Shorthouse** (…)
      a) **Coredelia** Holly **Shorthouse** (*1999)
      b) **Violet** Miranda **Shorthouse** (*2001)
    2) **Thomas** Percy Winkfield **Hughes** (*1974)
  b. Louisa **Hazel Agnew** (… - 15 Apr 1949)
  = 30 Oct 1913 London (dv.1926); **Sir Francis** Lynch Wellington **Stapleton-Cotton, 4**th **Viscount Combermere**, Baron Combermere, **9**th **Baronet** (29 Jun 1887 – 8 Feb 1969) son of Sir Robert Stapleton-Cotton, 3rd Viscount Combermere, etc.& Charlotte Fletcher; suc.father as Viscount 20 Feb 1898; he =2nd Constance Drummond
  no issue
  2. **Muriel** Helen **Goff** (20 Nov 1866 Dublin – 17 Jan 1951 Windley, Derbyshire)
  3. **Thomas** Clarence Edward **Goff** (28 May 1867 London – 13 Mar 1949)
  = 15 Apr 1896 London; **Lady Cecilie Heathcote-Drummond-Willoughby** (24 Jun 1874 – 27 Jul 1960) daughter of Gilbert Heathcote-Drummond-Willoughby, 1st Earl of Ancaster & Lady Elizabeth Gordon[35]
  a. **Elizabeth** Moyra **Goff** (30 May 1897 - Jan 1990 London)
  b. **Thomas** Robert Charles **Goff** (16 Jul 1898 London – 18 Mar 1975)
B. **Eva FitzClarence** (1 Jan 1847 Mapledurham, Oxfordshire – 2 Mar

---

[35] Lady Elizabeth was a first cousin to Sarah Gordon who married Lord Augustus FitzClarence

1918 London) (twin)
- C. **Beatrix FitzClarence** (1 Jan 1847 Mapledurham – 18 Mar 1909 Hastings, Sussex) (twin)
- D. **Augustus FitzClarence** (13 Feb 1849 Mapledurham – 16 Oct 1861)
- E. **Henry** Edward **FitzClarence** (19 Jan 1853 Mapledurham – 19 Feb 1930 London)
  = 11 Jun 1879; **Mary** Isobel Templer **Parsons** (1861 – 17 Jul 1932 London) daughter of John Parsons
  1. **Augustus** Arthur Cornwallis **FitzClarence** (16 Mar 1880 – 28 Jun 1915) killed in action
     = 7 Apr 1910; **Lady Susan Yorke** (7 May 1881 – 21 Aug 1965) daughter of John Yorke, 7th Earl of Hardwicke & Edith Oswald; she =2nd Wyndham Birch
     no issue
  2. **Cynthia** Adela Victoria **FitzClarence** (7 Feb 1887 London – 8 Feb 1970 Windsor)
     = 11 Jun 1908 London; **Roland** George **Orred** (1887 – 20 Jun 1963 Sunninghill, Berkshire) son of John Orred
     a. **Diana** Susan **Orred** (4 May 1909 – 5 Dec 1932)
     b. **Angela Orred** (*21 Mar 1915)
        = 11 Jul 1939 London (dv.1951); Lionel **Thomas** Caswall **Rolt** (11 Feb 1910 Chester - 9 May 1974 Stanley Pontlarge) son of Lionel Rolt; =2nd Sonia South
        no issue
- F. **Mary FitzClarence** (Sep 1854 London – 14 Mar 1858 London)
X. **Lady Amelia FitzClarence** (21 Mar 1807 Bushy Park – 2 Jul 1858 Hutton Rudby, N. Yorkshire)
  = 27 Dec 1830 Brighton; **Sir Lucius** Bentinck **Cary GCH, 10**th **Viscount Falkland**, Lord Cary, **1**st **Baron Hunson** (5 Nov 1803 – 12 Mar 1884 Montpellier) son of Charles Cary, 9th Viscount Falkland, etc. & Christiana Anton; suc.father as Viscount 28 Feb 1809; cr. Baron Hunson 15 May 1832; =2nd Elizabeth Gubbins
  - A. **Lucius** William Charles Augustus Frederick, **Master of Falkland** (24 Nov 1831 London – 6 Aug 1871 Tonbridge, Kent)
    = 11 May 1858 London; **Sarah** Christiana **Keighly** (14 Jun 1832 Madras - 4 Oct 1902 Kingsclere, Hampshire) daughter of Henry Keighly & Emma Huet; =2nd Boyle Vandeleur
    no issue

issue of marriage:
XI. **HRH Princess Charlotte** Augusta Louise **of Clarence**, Princess of

Great Britain and Ireland, Princess of Hanover, Duchess of Brunswick-Lüneburg (* & + 21 Mar 1819 Hanover, Germany)

XII. **HRH Princess Elizabeth** Georgiana Adelaide **of Clarence**, etc.(10 Dec 1820 London – 4 Mar 1821 London)

Selected Bibliography

Burke's Peerage Ltd. *Burke's Genealogical and Heraldic History of the Landed Gentry*. London: 1886-1972

Burke's Peerage Ltd. *Burke's Peerage and Baronetage*. London: 1840-1999

Cokayne, George. (ed. Vicary Gibbs) *The Complete Peerage, 2nd Edition*. London: 1910

Cooper, Artemis. *A Durable Fire; The Letters of Duff and Diana Cooper 1913-1950*. New York: 1984

Debrett's Peerage Ltd. *Debrett's Peerage and Baronetage*. London: 1899-2003

Dixon, Douglas. *The King's Sailing Master*. London: 1948.

Fox, James. *White Mischief: The Murder of Lord Erroll*. New York: 1982

Hart-Davis, Rupert. *The Arms of Time: A Memoir*. London: 1979

Hart-Davis, Rupert. *The Hart-Davis Lyttleton Letters*. 6 vols. London: 1978-1981

Munster, (Wilhelmina) Countess of. *My Memories*. London: 1904

Norwich, John Julius. *Trying to Please*. Mount Jackson: 2010

Patten, Willia S. *My Three Fathers and the Elegant Deceptions of my Mother, Susan Mary Alsop*. New York: 2008.

Tomalin, Claire. *Mrs. Jordan's Profession, The Actress and the Prince*. New York: 1995

Ziegler, Philip. *King William IV, The First English King in America*. New York: 1971

Ziegler, Philip. *Rupert Hart-Davis, Man of Letters*. London: 2004

INDEX

ABEL SMITH
  Samuel 130
ABOU DAHER
  Imad 120
ACKROYD
  Victoria 134
ADAM
  John 43, 127
  Thomas 127
ADAMSON
  Alan (1913) 122
  Alan (1938) 122
  Janet 123
Adelaide, Queen (née Saxe-Meiningen)
  16-19, 63, 111, 119
AGNEW
  Dorothea 185
  Hazel 186
  Henry 185
Alastair, Prince (2.Duke of Connaught)
  102, 172
ALEXANDER
  Sally 121
ALLEN
  Charles (Stuart) 64-65, 180
  Gillian 122
ALLGOOD
  Alice 154
  Charles 154
  George 154
  Guy (1892) 154
  Guy (1944) 154
  James 154
  Jane 154
  Mary 154
ALLYN
  Elizabeth 142
ALPIN
  Adrienne 177
AMARAL VALENTI
  Fernanda 131
ANDERSON
  Isobel 136
  James 135
  Liza 136
  Rory 135
  Thomas 135

ANDREW
  Rachel 178
ARBUTHNOTT
  John 171
Arthur of Connaught, Prince 102, 172
ASHCROFT
  Peggy 107, 176
ASTELL
  Isabelle 159
ASTOR
  Emily 135
  William 58, 135
BACON
  Katharine 179
von BAHR
  Jane 144
BAIN
  James 140
  Samantha 140
BALFOUR
  Annabel 178
  Ronald 108, 178
  Susan 178
BANBROOK
  Carol 147
BARCHARD
  Elizabeth 43, 127
  Francis 43, 127
  Jane 43, 127
BARFORD
  Amanda 469
BARNES
  Craig 122
  George 122
  Luke 122
  Thomas 122
BARSTOW
  Phyllida 177
BATCABE
  Michele 177
BATES
  Vanessa 183
BAYLEY
  Guy 166
  Inca 166
  Skye 166
BEEVOR
  Adam 179

Anthony 179
Eleanor 179
BELL
  Thomas 184
BELLAAR SPRUYT
  Andre 148
  Anneke 148
  Christiaan 148
  Nora 148
BELLINGHAM
  Anthony (8.Baronet) 81
  Augusta 809, 89, 91, 138
  Constance 146
  Edward (5.Baronet) 80-81, 138
  Gertrude 138
  Henry (4.Baronet) 79-80, 137
  Mary Emanuel 80, 138
  Noel (7.Baronet) 81, 146
  Roger (6.Baronet) 81, 146
  Roger (1884) 81, 146
  William 81, 146
BENDTNER
  Niklas 58
von BENECKENDORFF und
  HINDENBURG
  Herbert 104, 174
  Marie 104, 174
BENTINCK
  Anna 86, 150
  Brydgytte 84-85, 148
  Henry (11.Earl of Portland) 84-85, 149
  Jasper 86, 151
  Robert 84, 147-148
  Sorrel 86, 149
  Timothy (12.Earl of Portland) 84-86, 150
  William (Viscout Woodstock) 86, 151
BERKELEY
  Augusta 82, 147
BERROW
  Augustus 139
  Daisy 139
  Grace 139
  Joya 139
  Paul 139
BERRY
  Sarah 168
BERTIE
  Andrew 94, 142
  Caroline 143

Charlotte 143
David 143
Hugo 143
James 92, 142
Lucy 143
Peregrine 143
Rory 143
BERTIN
  Marie 157
BILLINGE
  Frank 181
BINGHAM
  Lavnia 153
  Suzanne 168
BIRD
  Christopher 151
BIRKBECK
  Edward 124
  Elizabeth 124
  George 124
  John 124
  Lucy 124
  Mary 124
  Nicola 124
  Oliver (1893) 38, 124
  Oliver (1973) 125
  Rosanna 125
BLACKMORE
  Susan 177
BLAND
  Anthony 177
  Dorothy (Mrs. Jordan) 14-15, 21-30, 31, 37, 44-46, 49-50, 77, 80, 111, 119
  Francis 21-22
  George 21, 27
  Grace (née Phillips) 21-24
  Hester 21
  Lucy 178
BLOMFIELD-SMITH
  Olivia 146
BLOSS
  Alan 162
BOEGNER
  Christian 99, 165
BONDE
  Augusta 35, 119
  Knut 35, 119
BORDEN-TURNER
  Comfort 107, 176
BOSTOCK

Petronelle 157
BOYD
  Alice 162
  Alistair (7.Baron Kilmarnock) 74-76, 161
  Arthur 162
  Benjamin 125
  Caroline 162
  Daisy 162
  Edward 162
  Florence 162
  Gilbert (6.Baron Kilmarnock) 71, 73, 160
  James 75-76, 161
  Jonathan 162
  Laura 161
  Lucien 76, 162
  Mark 162
  Phyllis 39, 125
  Robin (8.Baron Kilmarnock) 76, 162
  Simon 76, 162
  Timothy 162
  William 29, 125
BOYLE
  Albinia 168
  Angus 168
  Augusta 45, 137
  Cara 133
  Christopher (196-) 155
  Christopher (1992) 168
  Clementine 168
  Elizabeth 155
  George (1928) 168
  George (1999) 155
  Henry 155
  Jocelyn 168
  Jonathan 168
  Patrick 168
  Richard 168
  Robert 168
  Rupert 168
BRADFORD
  Francis 100, 166
  Jeremy 100, 165
BRAMWELL
  Anna-Rose 141
BRASSEY
  Robert 182
BRASZ
  Mirielle 148
BREAKER
  Gillian 122
BREMERS
  Emily 149
BRIDGER
  Julie 123
BRISTOWE
  Charleotte 184
BRONFMAN
  Edgar 99, 165
BROOK
  Sarah 124
BROOKES
  Carl 175
  Oliver 175
BROWN
  Anne 167
BRUCE
  Alison 141
  Jean 184
BUCHAR
  Namphon 146
BUDGE
  Caroline 171
BUDGEN
  Maureen 123
BULLOCK
  Harriett 183
BUNTING
  Caroline 173
BURROUGHES
  Pamela 163
BURT
  Christopher 127
  Jennifer 127
  Raymond 43, 127
  Stephanie 127
BUTLER
  Susie 160
BUTLER-ADAMS
  Fiona 131
CAMERON
  Allan 175
  Angus 175
  Arthur 175
  Clare 175
  David (Prime Minister) 105, 175
  Euan 105, 174
  Florence 175
  Ian 105, 175
  Imogen 175
  Ivan 175

Nancy 175
Tania 175
CAMP
  Sydney 179
CANN
  Michael 186
CANNARD
  Jacob 122
  Martin 122
CAPELLINI
  Antonio 99, 165
  Luca 165
  Luisa 165
  Sofia 165
  Vincenzo 165
CARLIER
  Stephanie 149
CARLINI
  Telma 139
CARLSSON
  Gertrud 120
CARLTON-SMITH
  Andreas 143
  Joshua 143
  Katinka 143
CARNEGIE
  Alerxandra 103, 173
  Cecilia 160
  Charles (11.Earl of Southesk) 102, 173
  Charles (Lord Carmegie) 173
  David (Earl of Southesk) 103, 173
  Finn 160
  Frederica 160
  George 173
  Hugh 173
  James (3.Duke of Fife) 102-103, 173
  Jocelyn 72, 160
  Maximilian 160
  Merlin 160
  Raymond 72, 159
  Willa 160
CARRINGTON
  Andrew 143
  Charles 143
  Georgia 143
CARTER
  Ivy 123
  Jane 134
CARTLIDGE
  Cecily 136

Edward 136
Samson 136
Wilfred 136
CARY
  Lucius (10.Viscount Falkland) 187
  Lucius (Master of Falkland) 187
CATOR
  Henry 38, 124
CAVENDISH
  Anne 58, 135
CAVENDISH-BENTINCK
  Victoria 184
CHAPPLE
  Rachel 166
Charles II, King 49
Charles (Stuart), Prince 64
Charlotte, Queen (née Mecklenburg) 7, 126
Charlotte of Clarence, Princess 188
Charlotte of Wales, Princess 15, 28
CHARRINGTON
  Edmund 185
CHESTERMAN
  Rosemary 163
CHIN-CHOY
  Helen 166
CHURCHILL
  Violet 126
CLARKE
  William 181
CLIFFORD
  Anne 178
  June 107, 176
CLIVE
  Virginia 135
COE
  Lucy 158
  Jennifer 158
  Peter 158
  Toby 158
COKER
  Denise 74, 161
COLLETT
  Philippa 136
  Susannah 142
COLLIE
  Jennifer 144
COLLOT D'ESCURY
  Andre 148
  Guyon 148
  Juliette 148

Marina 148
Willem 148
COLTHURST
　Oliver 130
　Shaunagh 130
COMBS
　Alison 100, 166
COMPTON
　Isobel 55, 131
de CONCHY
　Christiane 170
CONNELL
　Ciara 160
　Flora 160
　Jocelyn 73, 160
CONSTANTINE
　Annette 162
CONSTANTINIDOU
　Maria 129
COOPER
　Alfred 103-104, 174
　Artemis 110, 179
　Duff (1.Viscount Norwich) 108-109, 178
　Hermione 105, 175
　Jason 110, 179
　John Julius (2.Viscount Norwich) 110, 178
　Stephanie 104, 174
　Sybil 105-106, 176
COPPING
　Benedict 140
　Olivia 140
　Timothy 139
CORBIAU
　Simone 157
CORREA DE SÁ
　Antônio 136
　Inèz 136
　Marta 136
　Sofia 136
COUTINHO
　Sunil 122
COVENTRY
　Henry 140
COX
　Hilary 162
CRAGG
　Arnold 150
　Charlotte-Sophie 150
　George 150

Gulliver 150
Iris 150
Pierre 150
CRICHTON-STUART
　Alexander (1967) 144
　Alexander (1982) 142
　Alexandra 145
　Amanda 145
　Angela 144
　Anthony 141
　Archie 146
　Arthur 141
　Camilla 143
　Caroline (1957) 140
　Caroline (1984) 141
　Cathleen 141
　Charles (1939) 144
　Charles (1974) 146
　David 141
　Edward 145
　Eliza 141
　Elizabeth 141
　Fiona 93, 142
　Flora 141
　Fredrik 94-95, 117
　Georgina 141
　Henry (1938) 143
　Henry (2010) 146
　Hugh 142
　Ione 145
　James 141
　Jean 92, 142
　John (4.Marquess of Bute) 89, 91-92, 138
　John (5.Marquess of Bute) 92-93, 140
　John (6.Marquess of Bute) 93, 140
　John (7.Marquess of Bute) 93-94, 140-141
　John (Earl of Dumfries) 94, 141
　Katherine 142
　Kenneth 141
　Lola 141
　Margot 145
　Mary 92, 138
　Niall 146
　Nicola 144
　Ninian 143
　Patrick (1913) 144
　Patrick (1982) 144
　Philippa 142
　Rhidian (1917) 94, 145

195

Rhidian (1967) 145
Robert 143
Rollo 146
Serena 143
Sophia 140
Sophie 144
Teresa 144
William 142
CRITCHLEY
Ronald 174
CROKER-POOLE
Sarah 141
CROSSLEY
Julia 183
CUNNACK
Francis 185
CUNNINGHAME-DURHAM
James 100, 167
Nicholas 100, 167
Vioctoria 101, 167
CURRIE
Marie 158
van CUTSEM
Zara 152
DALY
Frances 22-23, 27
Richard 22-23
DANIELS
Rachel 165
Susan 142
DARE
Amelia 164
George 164
Henry 164
DARLOW
Ann 99, 165
DAVIS
Sharon 169
DAWES
Hermione 124
DAY
Hannah 171
DEASE
Mary 82, 147
DEFREIS
Arthur 151
Charles 151
Elisa 151
Graham 151
Lara 151
DENT

Lucia 166
Mollie 166
Piers 100, 166
DELVIGNE
Diane 42, 126
DEUTSCH
Anne Marie 163
DEW
John 181
DEWAR
Caroline 103, 173
DODD
Susanne 157
DORMER
Catherine 151
Charles (15.Baron Dormer) 151
Jane 151
Leanda 170
DOUGLAS
Hunter 163
Mark 163
DOUGLAS-DICK
May 154
DRISCOLL
Gaynor 145
DUCHEN
Andrée 155
DUCHESNE
Katherine 121
DUFF
Agnes 103, 173
Alexander (1.Duke of Fife) 101, 172
Alexina 110, 180
Anne 97-98, 164
Ida 101, 167
James (5.Earl of Fife) 97, 164
DUFF ARNOTT
Ian 105, 176
Neil 105, 175
Portia 105, 176
Tancred 176
DUGDALE
Charlotte 153
DuPRE
Joyce 167
DWYER-JOYCE
Susan 146
EATON
Suzanne 161
Edward VII, King 101-102
Edward, Duke of Kent 8, 16

ELBOROUGH
  Alan 122
  Amanda 122
  Anthony 122
  Bella 121
  Brianna 122
  Cadogan 37, 121
  Charlie 121
  Charlotte 121
  Daniel 123
  David 122
  Dorothy 122
  Edward 123
  George 121
  Heide 122
  Jasper 121
  Jayne 122
  John 123
  Jonathan 122
  Joshua 121
  Julie 122
  Justin 122
  Madeleine 121
  Mark 123
  Michael (1945) 122
  Michael (1948) 123
  Michael (1968) 121
  Natalie 123
  Nicholas 121
  Patrick (1920) 123
  Patrick (1937) 37, 121
  Peter 123
  Philip 120
  Roger 122
  Saffron 122
  Sarah 123
  Tobias 121
  Tonto 121
  Travis 122
  Wilhelmina 121
  Zachary 121
Elizabeth I, Queen 95
Elizabeth II, Queen 95
Elizabeth, Princess (Queen of Bohemia) 11
Elizabeth of Clarence, Princess 188
ELSMORE
  Warren 156
EMERSON
  Judith 151
Ernest, Prince, Duke of Cumberland 9, 16
ERSKINE-WEMYSS
  Alice 115, 184
  Dora 115, 184
  Hugo 115, 184
  James 114, 181
  Mary (ca.1863) 115, 183
  Mary (1885) 183
  Randolph 115, 183
  Rosslyn (1.Baron Wester Wemyss) 115, 184
ETHERINGTON
  Amelia 173
  Mark 173
EVANS
  Harris 150
  Ieuan 150
  Linda 144
EYRE
  Alice 82
FAWCUS
  Jeremy 175
  Molly 175
FAZAKERLEY
  Nicola 145
FEARNLEY-WHITTINGSTALL
  Sarah 175
FELLOWES
  Peregrine 151
FENTON
  Christopher 168
  Emily 168
  Peter 168
FENWICK
  Alexius 140
  Georgia 140
FERMOR-HESKETH
  John 135
FERNANDEZ
  Ana Maria 139
FETHERSTONBAUGH
  Birgit 155
FIELD
  Shirley 144
FIFE
  Alexandra, Princess (Dss of Fife) 102, 172
  Maud, Princess 102, 173
FISHER
  Ruth 162
FITZCLARENCE

Adelaide 35, 119
Adolphus 45-46, 180
Amelia 187
Annette 128
Anthony (7.Earl of Munster) 41-43, 126
Arthur 121
Aubrey (4.Earl of Munster) 36, 121
Augusta (1803) 46, 111, 180
Augusta (1822) 35-36, 119
Augusta (1823) 137
Augustus (1805) 45, 185
Augustus (1849) 187
Augustus (1880) 46, 187
Beatrix 187
Charles 40-41, 126
Cynthia 46, 187
Dorothea (1845) 46, 185
Dorothea (1876) 37, 39, 125
Dorothy 121
Edward (6.Earl of Munster) 41, 125
Edward (Viscount FitzClarence) 120
Edward (1837) 43, 128
Edward (1864) 40, 127
Elizabeth 45, 61, 64, 137
Eva 187
Finola 42, 126
Frederick (1799) 45, 137
Frederick (1826) 39-40, 56, 125, 128
Geoffrey (3.Earl of Munster) 36, 120
Geoffrey (5.Earl of Munster) 38-39, 41, 125
George (1.Earl of Munster) 14, 32-34, 119
George (1836) 40, 125
Georgina 43
Henry (1796) 44, 137
Henry (1853) 187
Harold 37-38, 124
Joan (1901) 43, 127
Joan (1904) 38, 124
Lilian 39, 125
Lionel (1857) 120
Lionel (1870) 40-41, 129
Mary (1798) 44, 137
Mary (1834) 125
Mary (1854) 187
Mary (1877) 40, 128
Mary (1914) 41, 128
Mary-Jill 43, 127
Sophia 44, 50-52, 55, 128

Tara 42, 126
Wilhelmina 38, 123
William (2.Earl of Munster) 36, 120, 181
William (1827) 137
William (1864) 37-38, 121
William (1868) 40, 127
FITZGERALD
  Henry 27
FLEMING
  Alexander 134
  Anne 133
  Edward 186
  Ian 57
  Joanna 134
  Josephine 134
  Lorna 134
  Philip (1889) 57-58, 133
  Philip (1965) 134
  Robert (1932) 134
  Robert (1998) 134
  Rory 58, 134
  Silvia 133
FLOWER
  Herbert 103, 174
FLYER
  Melvin 127
FOLJAMBE
  Arthur 152
  Edward (5.Earl of Liverpool) 152
  Hector 152
  Jemima 152
  Luke (Viscount Hawkesbury) 152
  Ralph 152
FOOTE
  Alice 181
FORBES
  Eileen 93, 140
FORD
  Dodee 23, 27
  Lucy 27, 80
  Richard 22-24
FOSTER-TOWNE
  June 182
FOUCHÉ D'OTRANTE
  Augustine 35, 119
  Gustave 35, 119
FOULIS
  Mary 52-53, 128
FOX
  Charles 44-45, 137

FOX-PITT
  Miranda 160
FRASER
  Poppy 183
Frederick, Duke of York 7, 15-17
de FREITAS
  Diane 155
FYSON
  Charles 147
  Erik 147
GAMBLE
  Fiona 124
GARNETT
  Andrew 129
  Michael 129
  Tara 129
  Walter 53, 129
George I, King 11
George III, King 7-17, 26, 45
George IV, King 7-17, 28, 34, 63
GILL
  Charlie 144
  Max 144
  Stuart 144
GLASSTONE
  Benjamin 129
  Ezra 129
  Rachel 129
GLENNIE
  Robert 151
GLUSKIEWICZ
  Adam 41, 128
  Anna 41, 128
GOCKEL
  Caroline 148
GOFF
  Elizabeth 186
  Ethel 185
  Muriel 186
  Thomas (1829) 46, 185
  Thomas (1867) 186
  Thomas (1898) 186
GOODFELLOW
  Susan 182
GORDON
  John 113, 180
  Sarah 46
GORE
  Eliza 65-66, 158
GRAHAM
  Sybil 158

GRANT GIBSON
  Diana 71
GRAY
  Lucy 162
GRAYSON
  Monica 41, 126
GREGORY
  Alan 135
GRESHAM
  James 163
GRIFFITHS
  Mark 163
GRIME
  Michael 186
GROSVENOR
  Dorothy 182
  Henry 115, 181
  Millicent 181
  William (3.Duke of Westminster) 115, 183
GRUFFORD JONES
  Flor 170
GUEST
  Rosemary 74, 161
de GUEVARA
  Cisco 179
  Rafael 179
GUINESS
  Elizabeth 68
GUNN
  Michele 177
GURNEY
  Jeremy 163
  Leo 163
  Luke 163
  Michael 163
  Mungo 163
  Rohan 163
  Rosa 164
  Stella 163
  William 163
HALES
  Catherine 153
  Timothy 153
HALL
  Kate 164
HARRENFELD
  Diederik 148
  Hendryk 148
  Hugo 148
  Wendela 148

HARRIES
  Alexandra 132
  Charles 132
  David (1938) 132
  David (2010) 132
  Henry 132
  James 132
  Lara 132
  Miranda 132
  Robert 132
HARRISON
  Anne 185
HART-DAVIS
  Adam 107, 177
  Alice 177
  Bridget 107, 176
  Damon 177
  Dierdre 108, 177
  Duff 107, 177
  Edward 177
  Eloise 177
  Guy 177
  Jason 177
  Louis 177
  Richard 105, 176
  Rupert 106-107, 176
HAWKER
  Martin 138
  Ronald 80, 138
HAY
  Agnes 64-65, 97, 164
  Alexandra 163
  Alice 64, 180
  Amelia 159
  Arthur 66, 164
  Cecilia 66, 164
  Charles (20.Earl of Erroll) 66-67, 158
  Charles (Lord Kilmarnock) 158
  Diana (Countess of Erroll) 71, 159
  Elizabeth 163
  Florence (1858) 66, 164
  Florence (1872) 164
  Francis 66, 164
  Harry (Lord Hay) 159
  Ida 64, 77-79, 137
  Iris 162
  Ivan 67, 163
  Josslyn (22.Earl of Erroll) 39. 68-71, 158
  Juliet 162
  Laline 159
  Merlin (24.Earl of Erroll) 72, 159
  Penelope 164
  Richard 159
  Rosemary 68, 162
  Serald 67, 163
  Victor (21.Earl of Erroll) 67-69, 158
  William (18.Earl of Erroll) 115, 61-65, 77, 137
  William (19.Earl of Erroll) 64-66, 158
HAY-DRUMMOND
  Agnes 103-104. 173
  George (Viscount Dupplin) 103-104, 173
HEATHCOTE-DRUMMOND-WILLOUGHBY
  Cecilie 186
HEFFLER
  Alexandra 126
  Leo 126
  Ross 42, 126
HENDERSON
  Edward 134
  Ross 134
HENEAGE
  Elizabeth 130
  Henry 130
  Thomas 130
Henry VIII, King 10
HESELTINE
  Silvia 57, 133
HETTINGER
  Caroline 139
  Charles 139
  William 139
HEYGATE
  Isobella 146
HILLIER
  Audrey 132
  Hugh 132
  Penelope 132
  Piers 132
HILTON-GREEN
  Chetwode 182
HINDHAUGH
  Elizabeth 177
  Felicity 177
  John 177
  Matthew 177
HIRSCH
  Nicholas 105, 174
  Richard 174

HODDELL
  Catherine 162
HOGG
  Eleanor 130
  Qunitin 130
HOLBOROW
  Benjamin 124
  Crispin 124
  George 124
  William 124
HOLDSWORTH
  Ruth 135
HOLMES
  Jasper 150
  Rhonda 177
HOME-RIGG
  Jennifer 140
HOPE
  Adrian 101, 167
  Agnes 101, 167
  Ethel 101, 172
  Mildred 101, 172
HOPKINS
  Jenifer 149
HOVELL-THURLOW-CUMMING-
  BRUCE
  Aubyn 170
  Miranda 163
HOWARD
  Judith 169
HUGGINS
  Lynn 178
HUGHES
  David 186
  Harriet 186
  Jesse 133
  Thomas 186
HUGO
  Tessa 168
HUNLOKE
  Alberta 134
  Clare 136
  Edward 136
  Delilah 136
  Henrietta 25, 136
  Henry 58, 135
  Joan 57-58, 133
  Matilda 136
  Molly 136
  Nicholas 59, 136
  Philip 40, 56-57, 133

  Philippa 58, 135
  Sarah 136
  Timothy 136
HUSTON
  Allegra 110, 179
  John 110
HYMAN
  Anthony (1928) 161
  Anthony (1962) 161
  Elizabeth 162
  Fanny 161
  Florence 162
  Harry 162
  Luke 161
  Max 161
  Merlin 161
INMAN
  William 178
INNES
  Phyllis 176
INSTRALL
  Mabel 123
IUEL-BROCKENDORFF
  Caroline 58, 134
JACK
  Theodora 128
JACOB
  Arthur (1867) 114, 180
  Arthur (1895) 114, 180
  James I, King 11
  James II, King 10-11, 64
de JANZÉ
  Henri 38. 125
JARDINE
  Michael 171
JAY
  Susan 109, 179
JONES
  Catherine 180
JOWETT
  Ingrid 167
KARUP
  Edith 170
KEIGHLY
  Sarah 187
KENNARD
  George 37, 123
  Zandra 38, 123
KENNEDY-ERSKINE
  Augustus (1866) 113, 180
  Augustus (1900) 181

201

John 111-112
Millicent (ca.1832) 112, 114, 181
Millicent (1867) 181
Millicent (1899) 113, 181
Violet (1863) 114, 180
Violet (1897) 113-114, 181
Wilhelmina 36, 112, 181
William (1828) 112-113, 180
William (1900) 181
KEPPEL
  Frances 38, 124
von KIELMANSEGG
  Alexander 136
KING
  Agnes 157
  Charles 157
  Elva 134
  James 134
  Valentine 134
LAMB
  James 154
LARSSON
  Judy 121
LAWRENCE MILLS
  Charlotte 42-43, 127
LAWTHER
  Elizabeth 155
LEE-WARNER
  Chandos 38, 125
  Jean 125
  Irene 125
LEGGE
  Octavia 166
LEITAO
  Felix 124
  Hermione 125
  Robert 124
  Tobias 124
L'ESTRANGE
  Mary 67, 158
LETHBRIDGE
  Georgina 153
LEVITA
  Arthur 104, 174
  Enid 105, 174
  Vioet 105, 174
de LISLE
  Arthur 169
LISTER-KAYE
  Amelia 150
  John (8.Baronet) 150

Melanie 150
Warwick 150
LOBB
  Henry 154
LOCKHART MUMMERY
  John 101, 172
LONG
  Ernest 183
LORD
  Alexandra 176
  Alice 176
  James 105, 176
  Olivia 176
  Simon 176
  Victoria 176
Louise, Princess Royal 101-102, 172
LOVELL
  Alexander 145
  Edward 145
  Henrietta 146
  James 145
  Nicola 145
  Peter 145
LOVETT
  Thomas 181
LOWSLEY-WILLIAMS
  Mark 142
  Michael (...) 93, 142
  Michael (1967) 142
  Patrick 142
  Paul 142
LUBY
  Elizabeth pp, 165
LUCAS
  Ruth 157
LUDWIG
  Susan 120
MacCARTHY-MORROUGH
  Sophia 156
MacDONALD
  Catherine 155
MACDONALD-BUCHANAN
  Alexander 183
  Archie 183
  Angus 183
  Flora 183
  Hector 183
  Hugh 182
  James (1931) 182
  James (1963) 183
  Matilda 183

Nicholas 183
  Orlando 183
MACK
  Richard 182
MacKENZIE
  Lucy 68, 158
MacLEAN
  Sophy 132
MAGOR
  Carolyn 134
  Richard 134
MAKINS
  Mary 178
MANNERS
  Diana 108-109, 178
MARCH PHILLIPPS DE LISLE
  Alexander (1896) 171
  Alexander (1983) 171
  Alexandra 169
  Alexia 171
  Althea 168
  Ambrose 170
  Bertie 170
  Bertha 170
  Charles 169
  Charlotte 169
  Christian 170
  Clare 170
  Daniel 169
  Dominic 170
  Edward 171
  Edwin (1852) 101, 167
  Edwin (1948) 171
  Elizabeth 168
  Everard 169
  Frederick 170
  Geraldine 170
  Gerard 170
  Hubert 171
  Hugo 171
  James 170
  Jasmine 171
  John (1891) 168
  John (1977) 170
  Julian 169
  Lancelot 171
  Laura 169
  Mary 167
  Maximilian 171
  Nicholas 171
  Peter 170
  Philomena 172
  Ralph 170
  Rosalie 170
  Rosanna 169
  Rudolph 170
  Rupert 170
  Thomas 171
  Timothy 169
  Zac 170
  Zinnia 170
  Maria, Queen (née Modena) 10
MARSH
  Fred 27, 29
MARSHALL
  Amber 145
  Brett 145
  India 145
MARTIN
  Geoffrey 127
  Isabella 144
  Lucinda 127
  Mary II, Queen 10, 84
  Mary, Queen of Scots 95, 116
MASON-HORNBY
  Catherine 143
MATZKIN
  Valeria 162
  Maud, Princess (Queen of Norway) 101-102
MAUDE
  Molly 70-71, 159
MAUNSELL
  Cecil 37, 123
  Cecilia 37, 137
MAXWELL
  Alexa 42, 126
  Bettina 145
  Clementina 145
  Francis 145
  Georgia 145
  Merlin 145
  Robert 145
McCOLL
  Helen 141
McQUAKER
  Rosemary 121
MEDRANO
  Jesus 139
MEEK
  Geoffrey 151
MELLOWES

Pauline 149
MERMAGEN
  Ella 144
  Jake 144
  Sam 144
  Toby 144
MILLS
  Charles 161
  Samuel 161
  Silvia 161
  Victor 161
MOITY
  Denise 146
MONCREIFFE
  Alexandra (1955) 73, 160
  Alexandra (1996) 160
  Elizabeth 160
  Euan 160
  Iain (11.Baronet) 72, 159
  India 160
  Lily 160
  Ossian 160
  Peregrine 73, 159
MONEY-COUTTS
  Crispin (9.Baron Latymer) 130
MONTAGU
  Katherine 59, 136
MONTGOMERIE
  Janet 143
  Philippa 95, 165
MONTGOMERY
  Alexander 169
  Edward 169
  James 169
  Nicholas 169
MORIER
  Victoria 115, 185
MORRISSEY
  James 165
MOUNT
  Mary 105, 175
MUNRO-WILSON
  Broderick 134
  Charlotte 134
MURPHY
  Hugh 120
  Thomas 137
NAISH
  Alice 146
NICOLLE
  Arthur 140

Dora 140
Edwina 139
Frederick 139
Hugo 140
Mamie 140
Miranda 139
NOEL
  Agnes 92, 147
  Alexander 155
  Andrew 156
  Anthony (5.Earl of Gainsborough) 82-83, 152
  Anthony (6.Earl of Gainsborough) 152
  Archibald 154
  Arthur (4.Earl of Gainsborough) 82, 151
  Arthur (1977) 157
  Belinda 153
  Blanche 79, 137
  Carola 87, 155
  Caroline 157
  Celestria 153
  Charles (2.Earl of Gainsborough) 78-79, 137
  Charles (3.Earl of Gainsborough) 79, 81, 147
  Charles (1885) 154
  Charles (1948) 155
  Clare 157
  Constance 79-80, 137
  David 156
  Denys 157
  Douglas 156
  Edith 79
  Edward (1852) 79, 152
  Edward (1886) 152
  Edward (1956) 155
  Edward (1960) 153
  Edward (2007) 152
  Elizabeth (1967) 154
  Elizabeth (1986) 155
  Gerard (1926) 82-83, 154
  Gerard (1955) 153
  Henry (Viscount Campden) 152
  Hubert 158
  James 156
  Jane 154
  Janet 153
  John 158
  Joseph 153

Julian 157
Juliana 152
Laura 158
Lettice 153
Maria 152
Maureen 52, 151
Norah 83, 147
Philip 154
Reginald 153
Robert (1888) 82, 157
Robert (1924) 157
Robert (1962) 154
Sandra 158
Teresa 157
Thomas (1958) 153
Thomas (2005) 157
Violet 152
William 157
NORMAN
  Mary 146
  Patricia 143
NORTON
  Helen 122
OATES
  Ophelia 135
  Thomas 135
OGILVY
  Angus 170
  Shamus 170
O'GRADY
  Joan 121
  John 122
  Linda 123
OPPENHEIM
  Christia 139
  Christian 92, 138
  Corinna 138
  Eduard 139
  Flora 139
  Maria Almudena 139
  Maria Gabriela 139
  Maria Manuela 139
OSTERGARD
  Cyrun 180
  Obediah 180
  Sophie 180
ORRED
  Angela 187
  Diana 187
  Roland 46, 187
PACKE

Ursula 144
PAGET
  Agnes 183
  Cecil 115, 183
  Henry 183
  Louis 183
da PAIXAO
  Edson 166
PARKER
  Rebecca 152
PARSONS
  Mary 187
PATTEN
  Elizabeth 179
  Max 179
  Samuel 179
  Sybil 180
  William 109, 179
PAULETT
  Lilian 183
PAYNE
  Charlotte 80
PAYNTER
  George (1880) 134
  George (1933) 135
  Janetta 134
  Yvery 134
PEACOCK
  Michael 134
PEACOCKE
  Barbara 174
PEAKE
  Mary 169
PEASE
  Carola 155
  Christopher 155
  Dorothea 155
  Edward 155
  Sybilla 155
PENN
  Fiona 184
PERCEVAL
  Ernest 136
  Ernestine 136
  Kathleen 56, 136
  Philip 56, 133
PEYRON
  Adine 120
  Carl-Gustaf 120
  Christina 120
  Edward 120

Elisabeth 120
  Frederik (1861) 35, 119
  Frederik (1923) 120
  Maud 120
  Sarah 120
  Victor 120
PHILLIPS
  Paul43, 127
PILKINGTON
  Iain 145
  Jane 145
  Kate 145
  Mark 144
  Rupert 144
  Simon 144
PIPE
  Lucinda 131
PIPER
  Katherine 184
PITMAN
  Veronica 154
PITTMAN
  Henry 154
  Luke 154
  Marina 154
PLEWS
  Doreen 181
PONSONBY
  Hermione 100, 166
POWELL
  Edward 123
  John 123
  Louise 123
POYNTON
  Chloe 127
  Jonathan 42, 126
  Oliver 127
PRIDDEN
  Agatha 153
  Benedict 153
  Charlotte 153
  Lucy 153
  Robert (1945) 153
  Robert (2009) 153
PRIMROSE
  Archibald (Lord Dalmeny) 182
  Albert (6.Earl of Rosebery) 182
  Helen 182
PUGH
  Harriet 132
PYNE

  Sarah 176
QUENTIN
  Marie-Dominique 171
RAMSAY
  Frances 53, 128
RATHBONE
  Alice 178
  Benjamin 178
  Charles 178
  Marcus 178
  Oliver 178
  Paul 178
  Polly 178
  Willow 178
RATTRAY
  James 130
  Robert 131
RAWSTRON
  Sarah 171
READE
  Catherine 157
REID
  Alastair 127
  Kerry-Anne 142
RENARDIER
  Catherine 171
REYNOLDS
  Kay 122
RITTSON-THOMAS
  Christopher 133
  Hugo 133
  Michael 133
  Rupert 133
  Theodore 134
  Walter 133
ROBERTS
  John 167
ROLT
  Thomas 187
ROSS
  Katharine 157
ROWLEY
  Caroline 171
RUSSELL
  Anne 147
  Brendan (1967) 147
  Brenden (+1956) 146
  Heber 147
  Hilary 147
  Nicholas 147
  Nigel 147

Patrick 147
Una 147
RYAN
   Dominic 163
   Patrick 67, 163
   Rupert 67, 162
   Siobhan 163
RYDER
   Jean 177
SACKVILLE
   Edina 69-71, 158
de SANDAGORTA
   Fidel 139
SANDBACH
   Emma 151
   James 151
   Samuel 151
SANKEY
   Hilda 127
SAN MARTIN
   Miguel 176
SCHOLFIELD
   Vivian 41, 126
SCOTT
   David 127
   Janet 184
   Juliet 127
   Maria 40, 126
   Sara 127
SHARMAN
   Brenda 122
SHAW-HAMILTON
   Oswald 147
SHEFFIELD
   Samantha 175
SHEPHERD
   Amelie 145
   Isla 145
   Tom 145
SHORTHOUSE
   Blake 186
   Cordelia 186
   Violet 186
SHOUBRIDGE
   Margaret 130
SIDNEY
   Adelaide 39, 51, 55, 125, 128
   Algernon (4.Baron de L'Isle) 53, 129
   Anne 132
   Catherine 131
   Elizabeth 130
   Ernestine 51, 55-56, 133
   Lucy 132
   Mary (1851) 53, 129
   Mary (1906) 53, 129
   Henry 53, 129
   Hilary 75-76, 161
   Philip (1.Baron de L'Isle) 50-52, 128
   Philip (2.Baron de L'Isle) 51-53, 128
   Philip (3.Baron de L'Isle) 53, 129
   Philip (2.Vicount de L'Isle) 55, 131
   Philip (1985) 55, 132
   Sophia (1837) 51, 136
   Sophia (1983) 55, 132
   William (5.Baron de L'Isle) 53, 129
   William (1.Viscount de L'Isle) 54-55, 129
SMITH
   Alexander 139
   Amanda 182
   Charles 182
   Elizabeth 182
   George 182
   Hugh 182
   Kaye 141
   Robert 172
   Sarah 182
SMOLLET
   Gabrielle 168
SOMA
   Enrica 110, 179
Sophia, Electress of Hanover 11
SOUTHERN
   Lloyd 122
SPETIA di RADIONE
   Dino 167
   Paganello 68
SPILLER
   Violet 163
SPOONER
   Pamela 126
STAPLETON-COTTON
   Francis (4.Viscount Combermere) 186
STEAD
   Clare 145
STEEN
   Inger 120
STEUART FOTHRINGHAM
   Alexander 156
   Charles 156
   Charlotte 156

David 156
Henry 156
Hester 156
Ian 156
Ilona 155
James 156
Lionel 156
Mariana 155
Patrick 156
Robert 155
Teresa 156
Thomas (1907) 87, 155
Thomas (1971) 155
Walter 156
STEWART
  Cherry 156
STONE
  Raphael 152
  Simon 152
STOURTON
  Mary 83, 152
STUART
  David 144
  Flora 144
  Rose 144
SULLIVAN
  Mary 158
SUTHERST
  Gwladys 98, 165
SUTTON
  Dinah 167
SWANN
  Charles 185
  Harold 46, 185
  Helen 185
  Karin 186
  Vanessa 185
  Virginia 186
TAPROGGE
  Silke 133
TAYLOR
  Jane 146
  Martin 133
  Matilda 133
TENNANT
  Vanessa 185
THOMPSON
  Blyth 185
  Denys 186
  Hannah 186
  Moya 186

Sonya 186
Vanessa 185
William 186
THYNNE
  Atalanta 136
  Cassia 136
  Lucien 136
TOWNSHEND
  Agnes 98, 100, 167
  Carolyn 99, 165
  Charles (8.Marquess Townshend) 99, 166
  Elizabeth 166
  George (7.Marquess Townshend) 99, 165
  George (2003) 166
  Isobel 166
  Joanna 99, 165
  John (5.Marquess Townshend) 97-98, 164
  John (6.Marquess Townshend) 98, 164
  John (1962) 99, 166
  Katherine 99, 166
  Louise 166
  Thomas (Viscount Raynham) 100, 166
TREACHER
  Michelle 121
TREMAYNE
  Benjamin 125
  Emily 125
  Michael 125
TRUSTRAM EVE
  Amy 177
  David (2.Baron Silsoe) 107, 177
  Simon (3.Baron Silsoe) 177
TULLOCH
  Collin 145
VEREKER
  Elizabeth 53, 129
  Jacqueline 55, 129-130
VERMEER
  Amy 148
  Fiona 148
  Nadia 148
  Paul 148
  Robert 148
  Romy 148
VESTER
  Nicholas 150

Victoria, Queen 8, 18, 34, 52, 79
Victoria, Duchess of Kent 16, 19
Victoria, Princess (German Empress) 19
VILLIERS
   Nicholas 131
VINCENT
   Katy 162
WAANDERS
   Bert-Jan 148
   Joep 148
   Norah 148
WADDELL
   Carolyn 141
WAKEFIELD
   Edward 131
   Emma 182
   Humphrey 130
   Maximilian 130
   William 131
WALKER
   Edward 138
   Hella 139
   Ione 92, 138
WALLACE
   Anna 135
   Hamish 135
   James 135
WALLER
   Elizabeth 156
WALMESLEY
   Edina 156
WALSH
   Cora 147
WALTER
   John 127
WARE
   Ruth 107, 176
WARRE
   John 134
WASS
   Nigel 31
WATHERSTON
   Patricia 156
WATSON
   Robert 175
WATTS
   Lily 143
   Megan 143
   Morgan 143
WEBBE
   George 164

WELCHMAN
   Diana 169
WELLESLEY
   Eva 183
WEMYSS
   Andrew 184
   Charles 116, 184
   David 184
   Elizabeth 184
   Hermione 184
   Isabella 184
   James 184
   Jonathan 184
   Leonora 184
   Mary 184
   Michael (1888) 116, 184
   Michael (1947) 116, 184
   Olivia 184
   William 184
WENDELL
   Serena 141
WENDT
   Steven 184
WENTZEL
   Charles 157
   Philippa 157
WERE
   Adele 154
WESTERBERG
   Dagmar 120
WHITE
   Annabel 169
   Anthony 168
   Charlotte 169
   Christopher (3.Baronet) 100, 167
   Jeremy 168
   Juliet 168
   Patrick 147
   Philippa 168
   Richard (2.Baronet) 100, 166
   Serena 169
   Sharon 147
   Zara 168
WHITSON
   Elizabeth 145
WIGAN
   Ivar 73, 160
   Michael (6.Baronet) 73, 160
van WIJK
   Selina 94, 145
WILBRAHAM

Alexander 131
Camilla 131
Jocelyn 131
John 131
Marina 131
Oscar 131
Rupert 131
WILD-FORESTER
  Nicole 140
William III, King 10, 84
William IV, King 7-19, 21, 24-28, 31, 37, 49-50, 63, 77, 111, 119
WILLIAMS
  Eleanor 127
  Peter 127
  Sophie 127
WILLIAMSON
  Andrew 150
  Arthur 150
  Elisabeth 150
WILLIOUGHBY
  Charles 133
  Charlotte 133
  Emma 133
  Flora 133
  James 133
  Michael 132
  Rose 133
  Thomas 133
WILLS
  Susan 143
WILSON
  Hilary 39, 125
  Suzanna 156
  William 101, 167
WING
  Frederick 40, 128
  Gertrude 40, 128
WINGFIELD
  Maurice 105, 174
WINNINGTON
  Sarah 152
WINSKI
  Halina 42, 126

WOLFERS
  David 178
WOLFF
  Tanja 149
WOLLERT
  Madeleine 120
  Ragnar 120
  Rolf 120
WOLRIGE-GORDON
  Henry 164
WOODFORD
  Theresa 122
WOODNUTT
  Jack 153
  Piers 153
WRIGHT
  Malcolm 122
van der WYCK
  Adriaan 85, 148
  Alexander 149
  Arnaud 149
  Caroline 148
  Dawn 148
  Douglas 149
  Felicia 149
  Gwendolyn 149
  Evert 149
  Maurits 149
  Philip 149
  Raina 148
  Rhoderick 149
WYNDHAM
  Mary 32-34, 119
YEATS-BROWN
  Sarah 153
YEVDOKIMOVA
  Anna 131
YORKE
  Susan 187
YORKE BEAVAN
  Winifred 129
YOUNGHUSBAND
  Eleanor 156
  Victoria 157

Other Books by Daniel A. Willis

NonFiction

Legends, Half-Truths, and Cherished Myths of the Drane Family

The Archduke's Sercret Family

The Descendants of Charles II
Volume 1: Monmouth

A Reference Guide to the Royal Families: What Every Reporter (or Royal Fan) Needs to Know
(Updated annually each January)

Romanovs in the 21st Century
(Available in ebook only)

Fiction

Immortal Betrayal

Immortal Duplicity

Printed in Great Britain
by Amazon.co.uk, Ltd.,
Marston Gate.